THE DOLLAR–MARK AXIS

THE DOLLAR–MARK AXIS: ON CURRENCY POWER

Brendan Brown

St. Martin's Press   New York

To Irene Brown

Contents

List of Tables

List of Figures

Acknowledgements

Many have spared graciously of their time to provide me with valuable insights into the functioning of markets described in this book. Robin Pringle allowed me to draw on part of my article of February 1978 in *The Banker*. Robert Aliber gave me the opportunity to present my analysis of zones at a conference at the University of Chicago. Leo Helzel supported enthusiastically my belief that a popular demand exists for study in international risk management. He both introduced me to foreign exchange dealers at The Bank of America in San Francisco, and promoted my work at Berkeley. Bankers in Amsterdam and Luxembourg discussed freely the mechanics of the international banknote market. Hali Edison made many helpful suggestions towards chapters 1 to 3, and gave numerical assistance. The American Express International Banking Corporation accommodated my research.

As with *Money, Hard and Soft*, this book owes its creation to the joint partnership of my mother, Irene Brown.

List of Abbreviations

CD	Certificate of deposit
CME	Chicago Mercantile Exchange
Comex	New York Commodity Exchange
Dm	Deutsche mark
EEC	European Economic Community
EUA	European Unit of Account
GNMA	Government National Mortgage Association Certificate
GNP	Gross National Product
IMF	International Monetary Fund
IMM	Chicago International Monetary Market
LDC	Less developed country
LME	London Metal Exchange
OPEC	Organization of Petroleum Exporting Countries
SDR	Special Drawing Right
Sw. fr.	Swiss franc
T-Bill	Treasury Bill
UK	United Kingdom
US	United States

Introduction

The myth of Sisyphus is a parable about futility. Sisyphus was condemned by the Gods to push a heavy stone to the top of a mountain. He knew that when it reached the top it would fall to the bottom, and then his labours would recommence.

Political initiatives in currency markets are futile if they amount to much more than an official stamp on developments that are rooted in the marketplace and the behaviour of transactors there. The future of the US dollar and how to create a zone of currency stability within Western Europe were the focal points of international monetary cooperation in the late 1970s. In *The Dollar–Mark Axis* it is shown how both problems were being resolved already by natural evolutionary forces in the world's money marketplaces. In a free currency market, unscarred by central bank intervention, the West European currencies would have tended to float together against outsiders. Diminishing international use of the dollar as a unit of account was not in itself destabilising, so long as the switch to other monies was symmetric for borrowers and lenders.

Dollar universalism of the 1950s and 1960s was succeeded by bi-polarism. Swings in the mighty dollar–mark axis cause orbital currencies to the dollar and mark to rotate also, although to a lesser degree. *The Dollar–Mark Axis* studies how currencies move in a bi-polar world. In chapter 1, the currency map is drawn, and the workings of axis power demonstrated. In chapter 2, the implications of zonal motion both for borrowing and lending decisions internationally are explored. The secret of dollar–mark axis power is the issuance of the two major international monies – the US dollar and Deutsche mark – by the largest economy in two different trade blocs. Chapter 3 depicts a kaleidoscope of the polar relationships that would exist if the dollar or mark were to be displaced by another smaller currency at one end of the axis. Could the Swiss franc, for example, become polar inside Europe? In reaching an answer, the comparative advantage of large relative to small economies in issuing an international money must be assessed.

Paper monies are creatures of governments, which are rarely well disposed to principles of free trade. Unrestricted tradability in paper monies has proved exceptional. Throughout the late 1970s, international use of both the Swiss franc and the Deutsche mark was cramped by central bank policies. Two-tiered credit and exchange markets, with the inevitably associated black market, are the subject of chapter 4.

Transaction cost considerations are the basis of many judgements made by operators in financial markets. The role of the market-maker in reducing transaction costs and promoting liquidity is examined in many different markets in chapter 5. The large share of the US in world trade and investment assures a high level of liquidity in dollar denominated markets. Innovations in liquidity creation, with special reference to the new currency and financial futures markets in Chicago, are studied. Too often freely floating currencies have been attacked at a macro-level for leading to high transaction costs and hampering international trade. In reality, at a micro-level, skilful design of markets and instruments can increase liquidity, just as engineering skill can reduce frictional costs in transportation.

In the late 1970s, a great expansion occurred in the international use of money. Less developed countries (LDCs) and other sovereign borrowers increasingly used the euromarkets as a source of financing. OPEC and tax refuge money had no natural currency home and were deployed in the four major international monies – dollars, marks, Swiss francs, and gold. The euro-banking industry grew very fast to service the expanding commonwealth of users of these monies. It has become anachronistic to discuss monetary policy solely in terms of national demand and supply for money in countries whose issue is used widely beyond the national frontier. In chapter 6, a synthesis is presented of national and euro monetary analysis.

The Dollar–Mark Axis is a companion volume to my earlier book, *Money, Hard and Soft* (Macmillan, 1978). Although both form part of a whole study, they can be read and understood separately. Both volumes share a scepticism of currency politics and are concerned rather with the science of money market structure. How should the investor or borrower choose between competing international monies, and how can each reduce systematically their transaction costs?

International currency history is still short. In the twentieth century we have seen the world's first international paper money – sterling – return to performing only domestic functions. Is it now inevitable that the US dollar will follow the same course, and is the Deutsche mark the dollar's probable successor? Or have we entered an age in which no one international money will be predominant? The answers must involve determining the bases of a currency's power to attract users worldwide. Currency power is the subject of *The Dollar–Mark Axis*.

Brendan Brown
January 1979

1 Currency Geography

FREEDOM IS NOT INDEPENDENCE

In the quest of a solution to the Grand Problem of the future of the dollar we must gain understanding of how the dollar numeraire achieved its pre-eminence in the contemporary international money marketplace. First we must examine the role of regional trade patterns in promoting currency power. Consider a world in which all currencies were unrestricted and floated freely without any central bank intervention. Currency motion would not be independent: for example, the Canadian dollar would tend to follow the US dollar against European monies, and the Dutch guilder would follow the Deutsche mark against the dollar. The movement of certain large currencies would draw other smaller ones into their orbit. The basis of such influence will be seen to be the trade and investment pre-eminence of the country of issue.

Terminology

Within the framework of currency geography a *currency zone* describes a group of currencies whose movements against outside currencies are closely correlated. For example, the Canadian and US dollars form a North American dollar zone, as they tend to move together against European currencies.

A sub-set of currencies within a zone may be especially interdependent, with their movements against others in the same zone being closely correlated. Such currencies are defined here as forming a *sub-zone*. The Belgian, Luxembourg and Netherlands currencies form a sub-zone in Western continental Europe, as they tend to move together against the Deutsche mark, French franc and Swiss franc.

A currency possesses *polar power* if it can dominate the movement of at least one other. Currency A is *dominant* with respect to currency B if currency B tends to follow A against other currencies, even when the source of exchange rate disturbance is entirely in A: yet the converse relation must not hold. For example, if the Luxembourg franc floated

1

freely, it would be an *orbit currency* of the Belgian franc *pole*. If a Belgian political crisis led to a fall of the Belgian money against the dollar, the Luxembourg franc would tend to follow, because so much Luxembourg trade is with Belgium. The converse is not true; a Luxembourg Government crisis leading to a fall of the Luxembourg franc would not influence greatly the Belgian franc, as Luxembourg trade is only a small share of total Belgian trade. The *polar field* of a currency consists of all its orbit currencies. In the five years since 1973, the Benelux, Scandinavian, Austrian, Swiss, Italian and French currencies have at times been in the polar field of the Deutsche mark.

Trans-zone exchange rates are those between two currencies that do not belong to the same zone. *Intra-zone* exchange rates are between two currencies that belong to the same zone. Thus the Canadian dollar/US dollar exchange rate is intra-zone, the US dollar/Deutsche mark exchange rate is trans-zone.

Zone Selection

When monthly exchange rates are studied for the 1973–8 period, two major currency zones may be identified (see correlation matrix in table 1.1). First, there is a North American dollar zone, including the US and Canadian currencies: second, there is a continental European (C.E.) zone, including Benelux, French, West German, and Swiss currencies.

Those two zones are founded on trade interdependence (see table 1.2). Two ways in which such interdependence furthers close correlation of exchange rate movements are demonstrated in the following two examples.

1. Trade interdependence furthers co-movement of real variables such as GNP growth rates. Hence greater non-synchronisation of business cycles seems possible between two zones, such as America and Continental Europe, than within the same zone – say between Belgium and the Netherlands. Out of phase business cycles can be the source of current account disequilibria: for example, faster recovery in North America during 1976–8 than in Western Europe was in part responsible for the remarkable swing round into deficit of North America and improvement in almost all European current accounts. Continental European currencies then tended to move together against North American ones.

2. Investment flows between the two largest international monies – the US dollar and Deutsche mark – further zone formation. Flight from dollars into marks causes the mark to rise and the dollar to fall

Table 1.1 Correlation Matrices 1973–8
monthly per cent changes

1. *French franc*

	Dm/$	Ff/$
Ff/$	0.5943	X
Ff/Dm	0.2576	0.0247

2. *British pound*

	Dm/$	£/$
£-$	0.2031	X
£-Dm	0.5269	0.0815

3. *Swiss franc*

	Dm/$	Sfr/$
Sfr-$	0.7557	X
Sfr-Dm	0.0431	0.0917

4. *Netherlands guilder*

	Dm/$	Dfl/$
Dfl-$	0.9079	X
Dfl-Dm	0.4955	0.2083

5. *Italian lira*

	Dm/$	Lira/$
Lira-$	0.1255	X
Lira-Dm	0.4876	0.1775

6. *Canadian dollar*

	Dm/$	Can$/$
Can$/$	0.1040	X
Can$/Dm	0.9066	0.0005

7. *Japanese yen*

	Dm/$	Yen/$
Yen/$	0.3622	X
Yen/Dm	0.4493	0.0357

Notes 1. Correlation coefficients are all squared, and entries above are R^2s
      2. Correlations are calculated for monthly percentage charge in exchange rates.

against other currencies. Neighbouring currencies to the mark follow closely its movement against the US dollar. The Canadian dollar rises little against the US dollar. The differing behaviour is explained by the comparative importance of Germany and the US in European and Canadian trade, and many speculators are aware of the exchange rate implications. A five per cent appreciation of the mark against both European and Canadian currencies would cause a much larger shift into

Table 1.2 Manufactures trade in 1976 percentage distribution of the merchandise trade (exports + imports) of principal industrial countries (columns) with 15 partner countries (rows)

	United States	Canada	Japan	United Kingdom	Germany	France	Italy	Belgium	Netherlands	Switzerland	Austria	Denmark	Norway	Sweden	Australia	Spain	multilateral shares
United States	0.0	84.6	53.4	16.9	9.6	9.6	10.5	5.5	6.2	9.5	3.6	5.9	7.0	8.8	27.3	17.4	15.4
Canada	39.2	0.0	4.5	4.0	1.0	1.0	1.1	0.4	0.5	0.9	0.7	0.5	0.9	1.5	2.7	1.2	7.3
Japan	19.8	3.6	0.0	3.9	3.0	2.6	2.3	1.6	1.9	4.0	1.8	3.6	7.1	3.5	30.3	6.4	6.2
United Kingdom	7.5	3.9	5.1	0.0	6.8	8.2	7.1	8.3	9.5	9.4	6.4	13.2	15.0	14.1	17.4	8.2	6.2
Germany	8.9	2.2	8.8	14.8	0.0	30.5	31.0	30.2	35.5	31.2	48.2	25.7	19.4	22.0	6.6	21.1	8.2
France	4.9	1.2	3.7	10.9	18.8	0.0	22.7	22.8	11.7	13.1	5.4	5.3	4.5	6.7	2.3	18.3	17.5
Italy	3.8	0.9	2.2	5.6	11.3	14.5	0.0	5.5	5.5	9.5	8.7	3.3	2.0	3.5	3.6	8.5	9.9
Belgium	3.1	0.5	2.1	8.4	12.6	15.4	6.8	0.0	18.9	4.0	2.9	4.9	2.6	4.4	1.7	4.4	6.1
Netherlands	3.0	0.5	3.2	8.8	13.6	7.2	6.0	18.2	0.0	3.8	3.9	3.5	6.2	4.6	1.8	5.1	7.0
Switzerland	1.9	0.4	2.3	6.9	6.0	4.2	4.6	1.9	2.1	0.0	9.9	2.8	2.1	3.2	1.6	3.4	6.4
Austria	0.4	0.1	0.5	1.6	5.9	1.1	2.8	0.8	1.3	6.7	0.0	2.3	1.4	2.7	0.4	0.9	3.1
Denmark	0.6	0.1	0.8	2.6	2.9	1.0	1.0	0.9	1.5	1.6	2.0	0.0	8.2	11.0	0.4	1.0	2.0
Norway	0.6	0.3	2.1	3.1	2.0	1.0	0.5	0.8	1.8	1.2	1.3	8.2	0.0	12.4	0.2	0.5	1.9
Sweden	1.7	0.7	2.0	6.0	4.4	2.4	1.9	2.1	2.6	3.6	4.5	20.5	22.6	0.0	2.5	2.3	1.9
Australia	2.6	0.6	6.9	3.0	0.8	0.3	0.8	0.3	0.4	0.7	0.3	0.3	0.6	1.1	0.0	0.9	3.7
Spain	2.0	0.2	2.3	3.6	1.4	0.9	0.9	0.6	0.5	0.8	0.5	0.2	0.3	0.5	1.1	0.0	1.8
Total	100.0	100.0	100.0	100.0	100.0	100.0	100.0	100.0	100.0	100.0	100.0	100.0	100.0	100.0	100.0	100.0	100.0
of which: with European countries listed above	38.5	11.2	35.2	72.2	85.7	86.5	85.3	92.2	91.0	84.8	93.6	89.7	84.4	85.1	39.7	73.6	69.6
Trade with 15 partners as % of trade with world:																	
1973	71.5	93.9	52.7	66.5	77.6	78.8	77.3	88.3	87.7	81.6	82.3	84.8	80.8	77.2	74.5	82.3	
1976	64.7	91.9	47.9	67.8	73.2	73.8	72.7	86.8	85.4	76.9	78.5	83.4	83.7	74.2	67.2	78.8	

Source: Morgan Guaranty

a each country's trade with the listed partners as per cent of total manufactures trade between the sixteen countries
Note: The table excludes invisible trade. Tourism, in particular, tends to be more concentrated regionally than is merchandise trade.

surplus of Germany's neighbours than of Canada. Similarly, a given depreciation of the US dollar against Canadian and European currencies would cause Canada's trade to shift more than Europe's into deficit. If Canadian and non-German European currencies were orbits of the dollar–mark axis's midpoint, Canada would be thrown into deficit and non-German Europe into surplus.

Trade interdependence is neither a necessary nor sufficient condition for the identification of a currency zone. The proposition is illustrated by two exceptions. First, suppose hyperinflation prevailed in Germany, whilst a firm monetary policy was pursued in Benelux and France. Then changes in the Deutsche mark would show little correlation with changes in neighbouring currency rates against the dollar, even when monthly rates of change were compared. The Deutsche mark rate would be dominated by daily rates of hyperinflation in Germany. Second, suppose Britain and Italy pursued monetary policies such as to constrain their exchange rates within narrow bands against a fixed dollar parity. Then we should observe a close correlation of the lira-dollar and British pound-dollar rates, despite Italy and the UK being hardly interdependent in trade. Indeed, it has been possible on occasions to detect a sterling-lira zone. For much of the 1970s the Bank of England and Banca d'Italia shared an intellectual framework of monetary analysis. They reacted to shocks such as the oil crisis in similar fashion, and quite differently from West Germany and Benelux.

A currency zone is defined relative to the interval of time over which exchange rate changes are considered – daily, weekly, monthly, yearly, or more. Where countries are interdependent in trade, but their monetary policies divergent, closer correlation will hold between monthly rather than between yearly exchange rate changes. Short-term exchange rate changes tend to contain a larger share of real exchange rate movement – defined as deviation from purchasing power parity – than do long-term changes. Where two countries which are not closely related in trade follow similar monetary policies, daily and monthly exchange rate changes are likely to be *less* closely correlated than 6-monthly and yearly changes. The latter are influenced more heavily by inflation similarities. Indeed, in the 1973–8 period, whereas the correlation (R^2) between monthly percentage changes in the British pound and Italian lira-dollar exchange rates was only 0.21, that between quarterly changes was 0.38. As already discussed, the periodic appearance of a sterling-lira zone was due to similarity of monetary policies rather than trade interdependencies.

Polar zones

For much of the 1973–8 period, the Benelux currencies and the
Austrian schilling moved within narrow bands of a Deutsche mark
parity. The Dutch guilder, Belgian franc, Austrian schilling, and
Deutsche mark could thus be regarded as forming an 'inner mark zone'
whose basis was both trade interdependence and the pursuance of
monetary policies designed to peg mutually these exchange rates.

In table 1.3, the trade relations of the inner mark zone with other
European economies is summarized. The share of French and Swiss
trade with inner mark zone countries is particularly large. Conversely,
the share of inner mark zone trade with France or Switzerland is
considerably smaller. The asymmetry is greatest in the case of
Switzerland. Whereas the inner mark zone accounts for 36.5 per cent of
Swiss trade, Switzerland accounts for only 4.8 per cent of inner mark
zone trade.

Table 1.3 Mark zone dominance 1976

	Mark Zone	France	Swi	Swe	Italy	UK
Mark zone	X	17.5	4.8	4.3	9.0	6.8
France	32.5	X	4.1	1.2	10.7	5.9
Swi	36.5	9.8	X	2.5	8.5	6.2
Swe	23.5	4.1	2.0	X	2.6	10.9
Italy	26.5	14.2	2.8	1.1	X	3.9
UK	20.6	6.7	3.5	3.8	3.3	X

Figures are percentage distribution of total trade (exports and imports) of the
listed countries.

Source: IMF Direction of Trade

It should be deduced that the Swiss franc – and the French franc to a
lesser degree – will often behave as an orbit currency of the inner mark
zone pole. A depreciation of the mark against the dollar induced by a
change in international monetary taste will pull the Swiss and French
francs closely behind it, but a depreciation of the Swiss franc against the
dollar due to a banking panic in Switzerland will have less pull on the
Deutsche mark-dollar and French franc-dollar exchange rates.

The polar role of the Deutsche mark with respect to the French franc
is greater than the share of the inner Deutsche mark zone in French
trade would suggest. Third-country effects strengthen the Deutsche
mark's dominance. For example, Switzerland is an important trading

partner of France. Because the Swiss franc itself is sometimes orbital to the Deutsche mark, French trade is doubly sensitive to the course of the mark on the foreign exchange.

The orbit-pole relation between the Swiss franc and Deutsche mark will hold less often than simple trade asymmetries suggest. Sometimes it is more appropriate to identify the Deutsche mark and Swiss franc as together forming a sub-zone among continental European currencies. Investment swings tend to occur between the dollar on the one hand, and both the Deutsche mark and Swiss franc on the other. The observed correlation of the franc and mark during such periods is due to common cause rather than mark dominance.

Zonal imbalance

Exchange rate determination is a multilateral affair. An imbalance in the international payments of one country must be matched by imbalances in other countries. Exchange rate adjustment will not be confined to the countries in which the initial imbalances are found: other currencies will be influenced differently, depending on their degree of trade or monetary interdependence with the countries in which the disturbance originated.

In theory, disequilibrium in one exchange market is resolved by adjustment in all N-1 exchange markets (where N is the number of currencies). N-1 equations, each including N-1 variables, must be solved simultaneously. In practice, exchange market analysis is an imprecise art, and the analyst must have a method of simplifying his work, whilst not denying the essentially multilateral nature of exchange rate determination.

First, simultaneity is a less significant problem when small currencies are considered. If estimating how far the Dutch guilder should fall against other currencies, given an announced decline in the rate of Netherlands natural gas revenues, feedback effects of currency movements on neighbouring states should be assumed small. Netherlands trade represents a small share of other countries' trade, and only a minor reaction of both the Belgian franc and Deutsche mark should be expected. In summary, small currency exchange rate fluctuations may be considered as occurring almost unilaterally: those of large currencies cannot so be regarded.

Second, when studying a payments imbalance which originates in a large country whose currency is polar with respect to others, condensed analysis of the payments position of zones is useful. As an illustration, the effects of two shocks to the international payments of Germany are compared. What would be the different impact on the Deutsche mark-dollar exchange rate of a 10 billion desired purchase of marks whose counterpart is alternatively a desired sale of French francs and US dollars? The desired switch from French francs could be prompted by a fear of a left-wing victory: that from dollars by a fear of an increase in the volatility of the US rate of inflation.

The French franc-Deutsche mark shift represents a purely intra-zonal payments imbalance, being confined to the continental European zone. The US dollar-Deutsche mark shift involves trans-zonal payments imbalance. The exchange rate impacts are summarized in figure 1.1.

	trans-zonal exchange rate change	intra-zonal exchange rate change
trans-zonal imbalance	X	y
intra-zonal imbalance	x	Y

note (1) x is less than X
          y is less than Y

(2) size of imbalance in
     each case is assumed identical

Figure 1.1 Exchange rate adjustment

The shift from dollars to Deutsche marks forces all continental European zone currencies upwards, with the Deutsche mark in the forefront. Yet ultimately, the current account of West Germany's balance of payments must deteriorate cumulatively to an extent equal to the desired given size of capital inflow into marks. Because the trans-zonal shift causes Germany's neighboring currencies to follow the mark, the rise of the mark against the dollar must be larger than if some of the currencies in the mark's polar field moved in the opposite direction against the dollar. Such divergent motion typifies the response to intra-zonal imbalance. The shift from French francs into marks causes the French franc to move sharply down against the mark, and also down against the dollar. Movement of intra-zonal exchange rates (specifically the rate of the French franc against the Deutsche mark) is greater, and that of most trans-zonal rates (excluding possibly the US dollar against the French franc) is smaller than results from the same size of desired investment switch into marks from dollars.

The differing exchange rate implications of trans and intra-zone imbalances illuminate a further force responsible for the appearance of a continental European zone in the period since 1973. The Deutsche mark is the major investment money alternative to the US dollar, and swings in international monetary taste increase the frequency of trans-zonal relative to intra-zonal payments imbalances. Disturbances which cause all continental European zone currencies to move in the same direction against the dollar are thereby more frequent, and the observed correlation of changes in their dollar exchange rates is so increased.

Trade-weighted exchange indices

It has long been realized that the current account of a country's balance of payments responds to movements of the national currency against the weighted average of those of its trading partners, rather than against simply the international numeraire currency. Until now, this has been the US dollar.

Although trade-weighted indices are an important input to analysing probable developments in a country's balance of payments, they are not usually the subject of speculative or hedging decisions. A French exporter must decide whether or not to hedge some anticipated Deutsche mark receipts. Therefore he must form a view about the path of the Deutsche mark-French franc rate. He might use an estimate of the movement of the franc's trade-weighted value as a stepping stone towards arriving at a final judgement about the course of quoted rates of the one currency against the other. But he must also be aware of zonal relations between currencies.

Even as a stepping stone, trade-weighted exchange rates must be trodden on with care. The most widely used indices – one set of which is published by the Bundesbank – are calculated using bilateral weights. The weight given each currency in the calculation of say, the Deutsche mark's index, is the share of the issuing country in West Germany's trade. Many of Germany's trading partners do not issue tradable currencies; others may export only one or two standard commodities whose prices are determined in dollars in a world market (for example, Chile's major export is copper). In the trade-weighted index, such trade partners must be awarded a currency 'proxy.' Oil and other raw commodity producers in the less developed world are treated as dollar countries in the Bundesbank's calculations.

Since 1973 – which is commonly regarded as the start of generalized floating exchange rates – inflation rates have diverged widely between the major economies of the world. Hence increasing attention has been given to 'real' trade weighted exchange indices. These are averages of the real exchange rate of the national currency with those of the trading partners, where weights are again bilateral trade shares. A real exchange rate is the nominal rate deflated by the relative movement of the consumer price indices in the two countries. Real effective exchange rate changes for the 1973–8 period are illustrated in table 1.4.

Table 1.4   Real effective exchange rate changes March 1973 to May 15, 1978, March 1973 = 100

US	−9.3
Canada	−6.7
Japan	+32.7
United Kingdom	−6.2
Germany	+0.6
France	−4.1
Italy	−15.6
Switzerland	+21.3
Netherlands	+13.0

Source: Morgan Guaranty
Note: Calculations are on the basis of consumer price indices.

Bilaterally trade-weighted exchange rates are subject to two major defects as guides to the effect of realized exchange rate changes on a country's trade. First, they do not take account of competition between two countries in third markets. Second, their calculation is not at all sensitive to inequality in elasticity of either export supply to or import demand from different markets.

The third market problem is illustrated vividly in OPEC markets. European goods compete with North American ones there, yet bilaterally weighted exchange rate indicators would not be deflected adequately by the likely impact of a Deutsche mark-dollar exchange rate shift on the net trade balance of both areas with OPEC. If OPEC currencies are proxied by the dollar in the weighted calculation, the US trade-weighted index, as an indicator to current account trends, would fail altogether to be sensitive to the likely effect of a Deutsche mark-dollar rate change on the US-OPEC trade. The German trade-weighted index would not be distorted similarly because OPEC is aggregated with US markets in its calculation. The German index is distorted as an indicator by other third market effects. For example, the UK trades more with the US than do other European countries. Therefore

German goods in the UK are exposed particularly to US competition and the dollar should receive extra weight in the German index over and above its US representation.

The omission of third country effects in bilaterally trade-weighted calculation is a very serious drawback to its usefulness where neighboring countries produce similar goods for third markets but trade little between themselves. For example, Greece, Turkey, Israel and Spain produce similar Mediterranean-type agricultural produce for third markets, which is for each their most important export. It is notable that the Bank of Greece, which fixes the drachma daily on the trade-weighted basis, does not use bilateral weights. It takes much greater notice of changes in the external value of the Turkish lira, Israeli pound, and Spanish peseta, than a bilateral calculation would suggest.

The second defect of the bilaterally trade-weighted index as a trade-flow indicator lies in the differing response of various markets to the same percentage exchange rate change. The US-Canada relation is used as illustration. Canada represents a large share of US trade: yet it may be supposed that a 1 per cent depreciation of the US dollar against the Canadian dollar will have a smaller proportionate effect on US exports to Canada, than a 1 per cent depreciation of the US dollar against the Deutsche mark on US exports to Germany. The difference can be explained by comparing the costs of exporting to the two markets. The costs of supplying the German market, (including transport, marketing and information costs) are greater than supplying the Canadian market. Fewer US firms have been able to cross the transport barrier to compete successfully in Germany than have been able to do so in Canada. A depreciation of the dollar against the mark has the potential to attract new US exporters into the German market. The same potential does not exist in the Canadian market, which is already almost 'home territory' for US suppliers.

During 1976–8, the Canadian dollar declined over 15 per cent against the US dollar. In consequence, the bilaterally trade-weighted index of the US changed by only 5–8 per cent despite many times greater depreciation of the US dollar against Japanese and West European currencies. The trade-weighted index severely understated the effective exchange rate adjustment of the US dollar.

One alternative approach to measuring the likely effectiveness of US dollar depreciation on US trade would be to construct a trade-weighted index for the US on the assumption that the Canadian dollar-US dollar exchange rate remained fixed. Predictions of the effect of the index changes on the US current account would be made. Then a separate calculation would be made of the effect of the Canadian dollar-US dollar movement on US payments. Together with the first calculation, the second would be combined to predict the total effect of exchange rate changes on US trade.

VALLEY OF IGNORANCE

'Happily lived mankind in the peaceful Valley of Ignorance.
To the north, to the south, to the west, and to the east stretched the ridges of the Hills Everlasting.
A little stream of knowledge trickled slowly through a deep, worn gully.
It came out of the Mountains of the Past.
It lost itself in the Marshes of the Future.'

So begins Van Loon's *The Liberation of Mankind* (Harrap 1933). Van Loon's chapter could open a book on 'The Liberation of Money'. From the end of the World War Two until the breakdown of the Bretton Woods System of fixed exchange rates in 1971, financial man lived happily in the peaceful valley of a world dollar standard. During those years, vague stories circulated about a previous period, the 1930s, when currencies floated. Destabilising speculation and damaging instability were supposed to have prevailed. The 'Old Men' in positions of power, warned against those who dared recommend a move towards cutting their currency adrift from the dollar link and floating. But then in the late 1960s the little stream of knowledge ran dry. Western Europe was threatened with imported US inflation. The 'Old Men' continued to warn against the dangers of floating, inflation accelerated throughout the Western world. By the early 1970s, international investors themselves came to rebel against the US dollar as their standard of value: increasing numbers started to diversify into gold, Swiss francs, and Deutsche marks. The brook of knowledge dried up completely: the 'Old Men' could not cope with the unprecedented investment flows out of the dollar and maintain the world on the dollar standard. The 'Old Men' who had earlier stoned those who questioned the role of dollar parities, now jumped on the waggon of those freeing themselves from the dollar. Official pegging of exchange rates to the dollar ceased in the major economies outside America, and then from 1973 monies floated. The two major investment alternatives – the Swiss franc and Deutsche mark – were so saved from the inflationary experiences of the American dollar during the latter half of the 1970s.

Beyond the dollar

In the age of Bretton Woods, the US dollar was the natural numeraire used in currency decision making. The hedger or speculator had to consider simply whether a particular currency was likely to change in dollar value over the period of concern. Exchange rate parity changes, when they occurred, were, with minor exceptions, unilateral. Further, the new parity would be fixed in terms of the dollar.

Today, when the major currencies are floating against the US dollar, the speculator and hedger cannot unquestionably select the US dollar as the best numeraire for their currency judgement. Consider the speculator in French francs who believes strongly that present expansionary fiscal policy will lead to a faster rate of deterioration of the current account of the French balance of payments than is generally forecast. He might suppose that, when trade statistics in coming months show his view to be correct, the French franc's trade-weighted value will fall to a level below that predicted by present forward exchange rates of the franc. (The forward trade-weighted value of the franc is taken as simply the bilaterally weighted average of the forward exchange rates of the franc with France's trading partners).

The speculator described wants to take advantage of his expertise in interpreting the effect of French fiscal policy on France's current account. But he may wish to avoid considering the broader question of whether the trade-weighted value of the French franc in three months time will differ from the rate forecast by the forward markets now. Other factors than French fiscal policy will influence the path of the trade-weighted rate over the next three months. For example, a greater-than-expected US trade deficit would result in lower-than-expected European deficits, and firmer trade-weighted exchange rates for European currencies, including the French franc.

The speculator should choose the numeraire for the French franc, against which to trade it, so that his position is least likely to be deflected from yielding a profit, should his surmise about fiscal policy and its relation to the trade balance prove correct. From table 1.1. it can be deduced that the Deutsche mark should be chosen as numeraire, and the French franc should be sold short against the Deutsche mark. Percentage changes in the French franc-Deutsche mark are much less correlated with percentage changes in the Deutsche mark-dollar exchange rate than are percentage changes in the French franc-dollar. Thus the French franc-Deutsche mark is less likely to be influenced by general trans-zonal developments (affecting both France and other

European zone countries) than is the French franc-dollar, or the trade-weighted value of the French franc. Thus if the speculator feels he has no above-average expertise in understanding general trans-zonal developments that will affect the French balance of payments, the conclusion above follows about the superiority of the Deutsche mark numeraire.

In figure 1.2 are summarized examples of choice of numeraire for speculative and hedging decision making. Some of the entries are detailed below.

It has been discussed already how both the Swiss franc and the Deutsche mark will be often the subject of investment inflows out of the US dollar. If a speculator believed strongly that the exchange market was under-anticipating the amount of disenchantment with the US dollar as an international money and that the Swiss franc is about to be pushed higher to an even greater extent than the Deutsche mark against the dollar, he would short sell the US dollar against the Swiss franc.

Sometimes, however, the speculator should trade the Swiss franc against the Deutsche mark. Suppose he has inside knowledge that controls on foreign purchases of Swiss equities are soon to be removed: that would be a development specific to Switzerland. Further, he believes that there will be no deterioration in the Swiss balance of payments that will be caused by events inside Switzerland. He would therefore short the Deutsche mark against the Swiss franc, as percentage changes in the Swiss franc-Deutsche mark are little correlated with the Deutsche mark-dollar. His expected profit will not then be threatened by trans-zonal payment flows affecting all continental European currencies about which he claims no special expertise in forecasting.

Separation of speculation on country-specific and zonal imbalances is more complex in the example of the British pound. In trade, Britain is less interdependent with its neighbours than most other European nations. Its central bank has often intervened in foreign exchange markets to steady specifically the dollar exchange rate of the pound. In table 1.1, it is shown that percentage changes in the British pound-Deutsche mark exchange rate have been more closely correlated than have been percentage changes in the British pound-US dollar exchange rate with percentage changes in the Deutsche mark-dollar. Thus it is not possible to exclude satisfactorily trans-zonal flows from affecting the outcome of a speculative decision by trading the British pound against the Deutsche mark. It would be preferable very often to trade the British pound against the dollar for speculation about British specific events.

	Deutsche mark	US dollar	Other
British pound		Effect on UK balance of payments of European zone imbalance	Effect on UK balance of payments of specific to UK development
Canadian dollar		for all speculation	
Deutsche mark		for all speculation	
Dutch guilder	Effect on Netherlands balance of payments of specific Dutch development	Effect on Dutch balance of payments of European zone imbalance	
French franc	Effect on French balance of payments of specific to France development	Effect on French balance of payments of European zone imbalance	
Italian lira		Effect on Italian balance of payments of European zone imbalance	Effect on Italian balance of payments of specific to Italy development
Japanese yen		for all speculation	
Swiss franc	Effect on Swiss balance of payments of specific to Switzerland development	Effect on Swiss balance of payments of European zone imbalance	

Notes (1) A 'specific to – development,' is a change in the country's balance of payments due to a factor which there is no reason to believe will be shared by neighbouring countries – e.g. a general election, fiscal and monetary policies.

(2) European zone imbalance describes imbalance in the national balance of payments that is due to factors common to all zone countries and likely to have similar effects in each e.g. general switch from US into European monies.

(3) 'Other' should be interpreted as a weighted average of the Deutsche mark and dollar. The choice of weights should be such as to make the cross rate of the British pound (or Italian lira) against the average as independent as possible of the Deutsche mark-dollar exchange rate.

Figure 1.2 Choosing the Numeraire

Sometimes, trans-zonal fluctuations of exchange rates will be particularly prominent, as during much of 1977–8 when the Deutsche mark-dollar axis was particularly volatile. Then the correlation between changes in the British pound-dollar rate with those in the Deutsche mark-dollar rate would be greater, while that between changes in the British pound-Deutsche mark and the Deutsche mark-dollar rates smaller than suggested in table 1.1. During such times, speculation based on expertise about UK specific developments should be effected by trading the British pound against both the Deutsche mark and the dollar. The proportions should be fixed such as to make the average as little dependent as possible upon the Deutsche mark-dollar rate.

Empty exchange rates

Speculative activity is concentrated normally on a few key exchange rates. Speculation must involve generally a polar currency. The Deutsche mark is the pole in Western Europe: the US dollar in North America and many other countries whose exchange rates are pegged to the dollar. A speculator in French francs would thus trade them against Deutsche marks or dollars, depending on factors described above. He will choose only rarely to trade francs against the non-polar currencies such as Swiss francs, Belgian francs, British pounds, Dutch guilders, or Italian liras. These latter franc exchange rates are examples of *empty exchange rates*. Speculation between the French and Belgian francs would not involve a pole: the French franc-Belgian franc exchange rate is more likely to be influenced significantly by developments in the Belgian balance of payments than the French franc-Deutsche mark rate by the German balance of payments. A sudden deterioration in the Belgian current account would lead to a fall of the Belgian franc against all monies, including neighbouring ones. The small size of the Belgian economy limits the power of its franc to influence other dollar exchange rates. In contrast, fluctuations in the external position of West Germany are very likely to cause neighbouring currencies to move close behind the Deutsche mark against the dollar. The impact of German balance of payments fluctuations will often thus be less on neighbouring currency exchange rates with the mark than with the dollar.

Hedging empty exchange risk

Much international trade in manufactured goods is invoiced in the currency of the exporter, at least among OECD countries. For example, French exports to Switzerland will be denominated typically in French francs. The Swiss importer must decide whether or not to hedge his invoices payable in French francs. The subject of his currency risk is the French franc/Swiss franc exchange rate, which is an empty one. If the Swiss importer decides not to hedge, he has judged that the product of the forward Swiss franc/Deutsche mark and Deutsche mark/French franc rates is greater than that of his own expected spot rates at the date of invoice payment.

If instead the common numeraire currency (see figure 1.2) had denominated the invoice, the need for a double currency judgement would have been avoided. Say, that the Deutsche mark had been used to invoice the goods exported to Switzerland from France. Then the burden of the two hedging decisions would have been divided between the Swiss importer and the French exporter. Each would have made the decision about the currency he knew best: the French exporter whether to sell Deutsche marks forward for French francs, the Swiss importer whether to buy Deutsche marks forward for Swiss francs. Specialisation of hedging into two decisions about country-specific developments is not possible in trans-zonal trade.

The choice of invoice currency such as to allow efficient division of speculative labour is no more than a slightly esoteric extension of Adam Smith's famous principle 'Each animal is still obliged to support and defend itself, separately and independently, and derives no sort of advantage from that variety of talents with which nature has distinguished its fellows. Among men, on the contrary, the most dissimilar geniuses are of use to one another: the different produces of their respective talents, by the general disposition of truck, barter, and exchange, being brought, as it were, into a common stock, where every man may purchase whatever part of the produce of other mens' talents he has occasion for.' (*Wealth of Nations*, Everyman, 1970, p. 15).

The mountain commeth to Mohammed

During the currency turmoils of 1977–8, the following types of statements were often heard: 'The dollar fell sharply against the yen in Tokyo this morning.' 'The Swiss National Bank provided heavy support for the US dollar as it fell below 1.8000 francs/dollar.' All such phrases ignore essential inequalities of size in currencies. They should be re-written as 'The yen rose sharply against the US dollar in Tokyo this morning.' 'The Swiss National Bank intervened heavily to prevent the Swiss franc rising above 1.8000 francs/dollar.'

Size considerations are discussed more generally in currency analysis at the beginning of chapter 3. Here, only the relevance of size inequality for choice of trading numeraire is posed.

In general, a speculator in a currency should choose as trading numeraire a larger currency. A currency is rarely orbital to one smaller than itself. What should the dollar and Deutsche mark – both numeraire currencies themselves – be traded against?

The Deutsche mark should be traded against the dollar. To trade it against a currency smaller than itself would transfer the subject of speculation to the other currency from the Deutsche mark. For example, the Swiss franc is unsuitable as a trading numeraire for the mark, because the Swiss franc-Deutsche mark exchange rate is more likely to be influenced significantly by developments in the Swiss balance of payments than in the German: whereas the mark-dollar rate tends to pull the Swiss franc-dollar close behind it, the converse is not true. Separation of the basis of speculation on the Deutsche mark between trans-zonal and country specific influences on the German balance of payments is not therefore possible (see figure 1.2). Any speculator in the Deutsche mark exchanges must include inevitably a judgement about the US balance of payments and how it will impact on German payments. The Deutsche mark's role as key investment alternative to the US dollar means that it is more influenced by US balance of payments developments than the size of the German economy would suggest. The counterpart of capital flight from the dollar is often inflows into the Deutsche mark.

We may describe the Deutsche mark-dollar exchange rate as the axis of the currency world. Speculative judgement on the tilt of the axis involves a perspective of the whole international currency market, and payments flows between its various zones. Speculation on intra-zonal rates calls on the skills of those with parochial knowledge.

The US dollar, being the largest currency, cannot be traded against any other single one so that the exchange rate is most influenced by developments in the US balance of payments. The US dollar-British pound exchange rate, for example, will be much more dependent on the international payments position of the UK than of the US. Taking a view on whether the dollar is to be weak (or strong) should be translated into whether the mark, yen, and Swiss franc, are going to be strong against the dollar. The speculator in the dollar, who wants to take a view predominately on the likely development of the US balance of payments, rather than on how US payments (together with other locally induced influences) will impact on one particular country, must trade the dollar against a basket of currencies, including the yen, Swiss franc, and Deutsche mark. In that way, the speculator hopes to avoid having to study local influences in smaller countries' balance of payments.

CURRENCY ARITHMETIC

In this section, two examples of payments imbalances between currency zones are examined. The first is capital flight from Canada: the second is an increase in the OPEC price of oil. Effects on intra and trans-zonal exchange rates are deduced.

Flight from Canada

Fluctuations in the international payments of Canada are capable of causing large exchange rate changes of the US dollar against currencies outside the dollar zone. Such potential influence of the Canadian dollar is based on the importance of Canada in US trade. The proportion of Canada in US manufactured trade (39.2 per cent) is much greater than any of the Deutsche mark orbit countries in German trade (the highest figure is for France, at 18.8 per cent): indeed the proportion, 39.2 per cent, is larger than that of Germany itself in any of its orbital countries' manufactured trade.

In practice, the Canadian dollar, despite Canada's importance in US trade, has assumed only rarely a polar position with respect to the US dollar. The explanation is that usually Canadian external payments imbalance has an intra-dollar zonal source, with its direct counterpart in the US. Fiscal policy induced current account deficit will be accounted for largely by increased US imports. Currency flight will occur mainly into the US dollar. In contrast, the Deutsche mark's polar position among European currencies was shown to depend on its being the main investment money alternative to the US dollar, and hence subject to considerable trans-zonal flows.

On rare occasions, however, the Canadian dollar has been polar with respect to the US dollar. In early spring 1978, the Canadian unit was floundering in the 85 cent range against the US dollar, having been near 1.05 US dollars two years previously. Capital flight from Canada into US dollars had been a major factor behind the fall. Many investors feared that the new Separatist Government in Quebec Province would succeed in breaking up Canada. On the assumption that capital which fled from Canada found its new home in US dollars, it should not have been expected that the Canadian dollar's fall should have dragged the

US dollar down against other monies. Indeed, currency flight from the Canadian into US dollars should have prompted a small rise of the latter against non-American currencies. The US dollar's rise would be small compared to the Canadian dollar's fall against other currencies, because of the very different proportion of US and Canadian GNPs that a given capital transfer represents.

In mid-spring 1978, the Canadian currency crisis became more than an intra-zonal affair. The Canadian Government arranged large foreign credits in Deutsche marks. In following weeks, large quantities of Deutsche marks were sold to support the Canadian dollar, which rose above 89 cents. The external payments of the US were not impacted upon by the Canadian intervention: this time its counterpart was in West Germany's balance of payments. Thus the trade-weighted exchange rate of the US dollar should not have been affected significantly. The large share of Canada in US trade implied that the Canadian dollar's rise should prompt the US dollar to follow, and that is what occurred. The Canadian dollar was polar to the US dollar.

The example of spring 1978 demonstrates how important a study of the Canadian balance of payments can be for analysing exchange rates of the US dollar with currencies outside the North American zone. The key position of the Canadian dollar depends on the Canadian Government or Canadian investors transferring capital between the Canadian dollar and continental European zone countries.

OPEC oil price increase

Most OPEC countries, particularly Middle Eastern ones, have tied their currencies closely to the US dollar: currencies such as the Saudi riyal have formed part of a 'greater dollar zone.'

Saudi Arabia's major export, oil, has been priced in US dollars, and its surpluses have been invested almost entirely in US dollars. Saudi Arabia's balance of trade is determined by world demand for its oil, the external value of the riyal having little relevance. The Saudi authorities, realizing that an active exchange rate policy would serve little purpose in this undiversified economy producing a standardised dollar commodity, have pegged the riyal to the dollar. Minor adjustments have been made when dollar fluctuations against European countries have been particularly large. Saudi Arabia's imports are bought both in Western Europe and the US. If the riyal-dollar parity was not revised following a sharp depreciation of the dollar against the Deutsche mark, the riyal price level in Saudi Arabia would jump. The riyal price of European imports would be immediately marked up, and such imports are a much greater proportion of the Arabian than US shopping basket.

How would a 10 per cent increase in the dollar price of oil affect the structure of world exchange rates, both intra- and trans-zone? The short-run effect on the current accounts of the main currency zones would be roughly as in figure 1.3. It is assumed that in the short-run oil exporters' consumption is irresponsive to their increased revenues, and that LDC governments are alone in raising foreign currency finance to meet increased oil payments.

		$ billion per annum
North American dollar zone	US	− 3.0
	Canada	− 0.1
Japan		− 3.8
EEC zone (excluding UK)	W. Germany	− 1.9
	Rest of EEC zone	− 4.0
LDCs		− 2.8
OPEC		+16.4

Notes: (1) figures are based on 1978 data
(2) Italy is here included in the continental European zone, as a large trans-zonal impact, such as the oil price increase, is supposed to outweigh factors that in more normal times cause the lira to be less closely related to other West European currencies.

Figure 1.3 Impact adjustment of current accounts to 10% oil price increase

An assumption must be made as to how OPEC would invest its extra $16.4 billion, given no short-run increase in its expenditure on goods and services. Suppose that OPEC decided to divide the surplus 50–50 between Deutsche marks and US dollars. Suppose further, that LDCs issued US dollar claims to cover the entire value of their increased oil imports. Resulting excess supply and demand of zonal currencies would then be as summarized in figure 1.4.

Exchange rate adjustments to imbalances shown in figure 1.4, are analyzed in two conceptual stages, trans- and intra-zonal. In the first stage, trans, all currencies within each zone move together, in reaction to trans-zonal imbalances. In the second stage, intra, currencies move against each other within zones and the trade-weighted exchange rate of each zone (see below) with the rest of the world must remain unchanged.

$ billion per annum

1. North American dollar zone	US dollar:	+8.2 − 3.0 − 2.8 = 2.4
	Canadian dollar:	− 0.1
		+2.3
2. Japanese yen		− 3.8
3. EEC zone	Deutsche mark:	+8.2 − 1.9 = +6.3
	Other EEC zone:	− 4.0
		+2.3

Figure 1.4 Impact excess demand for zonal currencies

For simplicity, OPEC expenditure is assumed constant throughout.

The trade-weighted (bilaterally) exchange rate of the North American dollar zone with the rest of the world is calculated as follows. The zonal exchange rate of the dollar zone with any one country, say Japan, is the weighted average of the Canadian dollar-yen and US dollar-yen rates, where the weights are the proportion of Canadian and US trade respectively in North American zone trade with Japan. The trade-weighted exchange rate of the North American dollar zone is the trade-weighted average of such zonal exchange rates, where weights are the proportion of each country in North American trade. The base Canadian-US dollar rate is equal to par.

Japan's trade is directed more towards the North American dollar zone than towards Europe (see table 1.2). Therefore adjustment to trans-zonal imbalance must take the form of the yen falling further against European than against North American currencies. The deterioration of the Japanese current account subsequent to OPEC's action is thus ultimately corrected predominately at the expense of the North American surplus: the reduction of the EEC zone surplus must to a large extent be matched in the North American dollar zone. Dollar zone currencies fall relative to EEC zone currencies, so inducing trans-zonal trade flows across the Atlantic Ocean towards America. Assuming that trans-zone adjustment is spread between countries in proportion to their shares in trans-zonal trade, intra-zone imbalances that would remain in the absence of second stage (intra-zonal) currency adjustment would be as in figure 1.5.

Where a country's payments imbalance has a counterpart within the

	$ billion per annum
1. North American dollar zone	
US dollar	− 0.2
Canadian dollar	+ 0.2
2. Japanese yen zone	−0.0
3. EEC zone	
Deutsche mark	+5.3
Other EEC zone	− 5.3

Figure 1.5 intra-zonal imbalance, subsequent to trans-zonal adjustment

same zone, less trans-zone exchange rate adjustment is prompted than when the counterpart must be identified elsewhere (see figure 1.1). The correction of the European intra-zone imbalance would likely require more appreciation of the Deutsche mark against the dollar than occurred in absolute terms during the trans-zonal adjustment to imbalance as shown in figure 1.4. The trans-zonal adjustment of the Deutsche mark in this second stage must be more than that of other European currencies in the opposite direction because Germany represents a minority of the trans-zonal trade of the EEC, and the zone's trade-weighted exchange rate must be unchanged. In North America, the US dollar makes negligible adjustment on a trans-zonal trade-weighted basis, whilst the Canadian dollar will appreciate against the US dollar.

Fitting exchange rate adjustment in stages one and two together, the final outcome may be examined qualitatively. The US dollar will have fallen against the Deutsche mark, but will probably have risen against the other European currencies and will certainly have risen against the Japanese yen by a substantial amount. The yen will have fallen against all currencies, both in Europe and North America. The special situation of North European oil producers, the UK and Norway, is not considered here.

CURRENCY AREAS, BLOCS AND ZONES

The identification of currency zones and poles in the context of floating exchange rates has become possible only since the breakdown of the Bretton Woods system in 1971. However the forces of investment and trade dominance whose effects are now explicit in the pattern of exchange motion were previously effective politically in persuading governments of small currencies to form fixed exchange rate blocs around their largest trade partner. The gold bloc of the 1930s, then the sterling area, then the universal dollar area, then regional blocs found in the post 1971 era, are taken here as examples.

Gold bloc

After the British and American departure from the Gold Standard in 1931 and 1933 respectively, a 'gold bloc' was formalized in 1933 among the chief European countries who continued to peg their currencies to gold. Included were France, Switzerland, Belgium, the Netherlands, Luxembourg, Italy, Poland, and the Free City of Danzig. The currencies of the last three states became quickly victims to spreading inconvertibility. The remaining countries were identical to the present members of the continental European zone, with the obvious exception of Germany.

Belgium was the first country to defect from its gold parity, in 1935, when it devalued the franc by 28 per cent. The country had been particularly badly hit by the world depression, as her exports were composed largely of heavy industrial goods, most prominently iron and steel. Though causing transitory jitters in the exchange markets of other gold bloc countries, none followed the Belgian move. Belgium was (and is) a small economy, and its currency was not polar with respect to any other.

In September 1936, the French franc was devalued by about 36 per cent. Economic depression in France and political anxieties had spurred capital flight on an immense scale. Unlike for Belgium, the French franc move was followed within a few days by similar sized devaluations of the Swiss franc and Netherlands guilder. The large share of France in the external trade of these countries helps to explain that polar power of the French franc.

By end September 1936, a gold bloc was again apparent, with the Benelux currencies, Swiss and French francs pegged to gold. The new bloc did not have a long life. In June 1937, the French franc embarked on an eleven-month float. This time the Swiss franc and Benelux currencies did not follow: the respective governments chose to remain tied to gold rather than risk the inflationary consequences of following the French move. The promptings of trade interdependence were overruled by considerations of monetary rectitude.

From May 1938 until the outbreak of World War Two, the French franc was pegged to sterling. During much of the remainder of 1938 both sterling and the French franc slid against the US dollar, as fears of a European war provoked capital flight from both Britain and France. So France became a member of the sterling bloc. The choice of the sterling peg was attributable in part to the growing similarity of capital imbalance in French and British payments, in both cases being essentially trans-zonal, and occurring simultaneously.

Sterling bloc 1930s

The sterling bloc grew in the wake of Britain's departure from the Gold Standard. The sterling bloc in the 1930s was purely an arrangement 'de convenance'; it was an informal grouping of countries with mutually close commercial and financial connections. Britain was usually the most important country in bloc members' trade, and in a free float sterling would often have been polar with respect to other currencies in the bloc. In reality, sterling bloc countries pegged their currencies' exchange rate to sterling. Investment links were close between sterling bloc countries and Britain. Both private individuals and institutions throughout the sterling bloc tended to hold their monetary assets and liabilities in sterling denomination.

In September 1931, the first entrants to the sterling bloc were the Colonies and Dominions (with the important exception of Canada), Ireland, Portugal, Scandinavia, Latvia, Estonia, and Iran. Canada chose to remain tied to the US in currency affairs, due to evident trade and investment interdependence with its large neighbour.

Sterling area

In 1939, September, the sterling bloc gave way to the sterling area. A currency 'area' is distinct from a currency 'bloc'. A currency area is a group of countries who not only peg their mutual exchange rates but also agree not to administer exchange controls with respect to each other: usually the country with the most rigorous controls will require others to police evasion via their territories. Often membership is conditional on standardisation of controls with respect to non-area members: such was the case with the sterling area, born in September 1939. Several countries dropped their association then with sterling, prefering to retain convertibility and forego the benefits of unrestricted bilateral payments from the UK. Scandinavian countries, in particular, unpegged their currencies from sterling. In general, states with the

The Dollar–Mark Axis

loosest political and economic association to the UK broke their sterling link.

Sterling has remained partially inconvertible, in varying degrees, since 1939. By 1978 only Eire and certain minor island dependencies remained in the sterling area. The importance of the UK in world trade had diminished to such an extent, and its inflationary performance had become so uncertain, that few countries could gain from pegging their currencies to the British pound.

The decline in the polar power of the British pound, and hence the reduced incentive for countries to remain in the sterling area, can be deduced from the number of countries that followed the 1949 and 1967 devaluations of sterling, (see table 1.5). Whereas in 1949 most of

Table 1.5   Declining Polar Power of British Pound 1949–67

1. Non-commonwealth countries who followed UK's devaluation of 30.5 % against the dollar 1949, and amount.

Austria	30.6 %	Indonesia	30.2
Belgium	12.3	Israel	30.5
Canada	9.1	Italy	8.0
Denmark	30.5	Luxembourg	12.3
Egypt	30.5	Netherlands	30.3
Finland	30.4	Norway	30.5
France	38.6	Portugal	13.0
Germany	20.6	Sweden	20.5
Greece	33.3	Thailand	20.0

2. Non-commonwealth countries who followed UK's devaluation of 14 % against the dollar 1967, and amount.

Brazil	15.7
Denmark	7.9
Israel	14.3
Macao	5.7
Nepal	24.75
Spain	14.3

Source: Benjamin Cohe
The Future of Sterlir
(Macmillan: 1971

Western Europe followed the British devaluation, in 1967 only Denmark and Spain did – both countries with particularly close commercial ties to the UK.

Universal dollar bloc, 1957–71

The restoration of non-resident convertibility for most West European monies can be dated back to 1957. In the subsequent period to 1971, the developed world could have been described as forming a dollar bloc. Exchange rates were fixed against the dollar, and the US guaranteed convertibility of the dollar into gold at a fixed parity. That pledge was the basis of European and Japanese Governments being willing to use a dollar peg. Gold convertibility was viewed as the ultimate brake on US inflationary tendencies. When that brake was removed in August 1971, key European Governments chose no longer to follow blindly US monetary policy, and by 1973 the practice of generalized floating had set in.

In the last years of the universal dollar bloc, the nascent polar power of the Deutsche mark was demonstrated on occasion. For example, when the Deutsche mark was revalued against the dollar by 5 per cent in 1961, the Netherlands revalued the guilder by the same amount the following day. The Swiss and French francs came under intense upward pressure in following days, but central bank intervention successfully kept the lid on the official dollar parity ceiling. Sterling was subject to considerable bear pressure, in part due to its then not very important trade links with continental Europe and its greater interdependence with American and sterling area trade.

Regional currency blocs, 1973–

The universal dollar bloc of the late 1950s and 60s gave way to floating of the major currencies, with smaller ones tending to form a bloc around the regional pole. The two main blocs have been the dollar bloc and the European Snake. The dollar bloc contains countries such as Thailand, Venezuela, and several Carribean and Pacific states, that express their exchange rate parities in terms of the dollar, and pursue a fixed or adjustable peg exchange rate policy. The European Snake has included West Germany, Benelux, Denmark, Sweden, Norway, and France (albeit some intermittently). The French franc has been floating for much of the post 1973 period, whilst Austria has pegged the schilling to the mark.

Smaller currency blocs have persisted, mostly satisfying the stricter definition of currency area. A French franc area including France's ex-African colonies, a sterling area including Eire, and Belgian franc area including Luxembourg are all exchange control free areas as well as fixed exchange rate blocs. Minor examples of areas include Switzerland–Lichtenstein, and South Africa–Botswana.

Is investment fashion regional?

A distinguishing feature of currency blocs has been that smaller member Governments have held their reserves largely in the dominant money of the bloc. Both the gold bloc of the 1930s and the Deutsche mark bloc of the 1970s have been uncharacteristic in that respect.

Though France was the largest member of the gold bloc, and the French franc proved polar with respect to the smaller members, the latter did not hold reserves in French francs. Each currency was fixed against gold, and reserves were held predominately in that metal. The French franc did not enjoy sufficient monetary or political confidence to become a reserve money, despite being the largest currency still tied to gold.

In the 1970s, reserves within the European Snake were held predominately in gold or US dollars. The Deutsche mark was used mainly as an intervention money, obtainable via the swap lines with the Bundesbank. The sluggishness with which the Deutsche mark grew in the reserves of mark bloc governments was attributable to three major factors. First, a large 'overhang' of dollars persisted in member reserves from the fifteen years of their dollar bloc affiliation. Second, the Bundesbank has pursued a policy of mild currency nationalism. Whilst happy to arrange swap lines in marks to preserve fixed rates within the Snake, the Bundesbank has been reluctant to see the mark play an increased reserve role. Third, an overhang of political considerations has made European Governments cautious about extending rapidly mark representation in their reserves.

At the level of private investment and borrowing, the Deutsche mark has gained in importance, particularly within the continental European zone. Whereas both the Banca d'Italia and the Bank of England throughout much of the 1970s continued to borrow and invest almost entirely in US dollars, the residents of the two countries were quicker to change their currency preferences. The greater use of the Deutsche mark to denominate international borrowing within Europe than outside is illustrated in table 1.6. From table 1.6 the observation can be made that Austria, Denmark, the Netherlands and Norway were the most intensive borrowers of Deutsche marks. The finding is not surprising: for much of the 1970s the currencies of these countries were floating against the Deutsche mark within only narrow bands. Hence

Table 1.6   Public bond offerings, 1976

	$ million denominated in	
	US dollar	Deutsche mark
1. Western Europe		
Luxembourg	355	67
Austria	290	337
Denmark	145	218
Finland	130	–
France	805	210
Italy	180	–
Netherlands	185	178
Norway	470	430
Sweden	750	160
United Kingdom	1305	139
Germany	260	–
Total	4875	1739
2. European International Organizations		
	1260	248
3. Rest of developed world		
New Zealand	175	125
Australia	604	–
Canada	950	340
Japan	855	229
US	1165	10
	3749	704

Source: World Bank

residents in these countries exposed themselves to little exchange risk by borrowing Deutsche marks rather than their own currency.

Within a currency bloc, the risk advantages of borrowing the dominant currency compared to non-member currencies are intuitive. More ambiguous is the choice of international money for residents of a country, which though belonging to a currency zone does not form part of a currency bloc. France, for example, for most of 1976–8, was not a part of the European Snake. Yet weekly, monthly, and quarterly changes in the French franc-dollar and Deutsche mark-dollar exchange rates were closely correlated. When the envisaged international borrowing or lending is for only a short duration, the polar currency of the zone, the Deutsche mark, is likely to be less volatile than the US dollar in terms of the French franc, and should hence often be preferred as a unit of account.

Over longer periods of time, exchange rate correlation between currencies depends more on similarity of monetary policies and less on trade interdependencies. When six-monthly, or greater, exchange rate changes are examined, the volatility of the French franc-dollar exchange rate could often be less than that of the French franc-Deutsche mark exchange rate. In the 1973–8 period, the French inflation rate persistently exceeded that in the US (whose rate in turn exceeded the West German one). Trade interdependencies would prompt the real French franc-dollar exchange rate to move in similar direction to the real Deutsche mark-dollar exchange rate, during periods in which the Deutsche mark was most influenced by trans-zonal imbalances. Inflation differentials could prevent the nominal dollar exchange rates of the French franc and Deutsche mark being correlated over long periods of time.

Further, an arithmetic note of warning should be sounded. Even if significant correlation is found between, say, quarterly *rates of change* of the French franc-dollar and Deutsche mark-dollar exchange rate, it does not follow that the volatility of the French franc-dollar rate is less than that of the French franc-Deutsche mark rate, where end-quarter observations are used. It can however be stated that the closer the correlation between the rate of change of the two dollar exchange rates, and the shorter the period being considered, the more likely it is that the volatility of the cross exchange rate (Deutsche mark-French franc) will be less than of the respective dollar exchange rates.

CURRENCY AND PHYSICAL GEOGRAPHY COMPARED

During periods when trans-zonal imbalances are large, exchange rate correlation increases within the zone, and indeed the geographic boundary of the zone should be extended. The use of the dominant currency of the zone would then increase in popularity for short-term borrowing and lending by the extended zone members.

For example, whereas the rate of change of the British pound-US dollar exchange rate is often not closely related to that of the Deutsche mark-dollar, during the dollar crisis of winter 1977–8, the correlation of short-term rates was high. Mapping of currency zones is analogous to mapping zones of precipitation and temperature in physical geography.

At different seasons, the same country belongs to different temperature and precipitation zones. In currency geography, mapping must be in part impressionistic. Periods of large trans-zonal imbalance do not alternate with trans-zonal balance in a regular fashion. The currency geographer must first determine what season he is in before charting his zones.

Political boundaries break many economic regions into several parts. Currency usage changes at frontiers, and large exchange rate changes are thus possible between different parts of the same region. How could a world in which currency usage was determined regionally rather than politically differ from the present?

The three faces of Mont Blanc

Mont Blanc extends across three frontiers. One major tourist centre is found on each slope: Chamonix in France, Aosta in Italy, and Martigny in Switzerland. Each centre competes in offering Alpine holidays. Yet the fluctuations in the real exchange rates of the French franc, Italian lira, and Swiss franc against each other have been very large in the post-1973 era.

The trade interdependence of Alpine France, Alpine Italy, and French Switzerland, is evidently greater than that of France, Italy, and Switzerland considered as whole nations. If each Alpine district had had its own currency, the rate of change over short intervals of the three against the dollar would have been much closer than that of the dollar exchange rates of the French franc, Italian lira, and Swiss franc.

Let us define the real dollar exchange rate of Alpine France as the rate of exchange of the French franc deflated by the consumer price index in Alpine France against the US dollar deflated by the consumer price index in the US. The real dollar exchange rates of Alpine Italy and French Switzerland are defined similarly. Regional trade interdependence should cause the rate of change of the real dollar exchange rate of Alpine France to be more closely correlated with that of Alpine Italy, or French Switzerland, than is the case between the respective national real dollar exchange rates. The mechanism by which regional real exchange rate movement is differentiated from national is consumer price index movements differing between different regions in the same state. Local evidence suggests that consumer prices in Alpine France rose during the late seventies at a faster rate than in the French interior. The real depreciation of the Alpine franc against the Swiss franc has thus been less than that of the French franc.

Alsace and the Rhineland

Alsace, the most eastern of French provinces, has for centuries been of ambiguous nationhood. For most of the twentieth century it has formed part of France. Yet a much larger share of Alsace's extra-regional trade is with Germany than for other French regions. Thus a given depreciation of the French franc against the Deutsche mark implies a larger trade-weighted depreciation of the Alsatian franc than interior region French francs: all regional francs are of course identically interchangeable at par.

Yet let us assume that the Deutsche mark rise was in no way attributable to a payments imbalance that had a disproportionate share of its counterpart in the external payments of the Alsace region. Then the effective (real trade-weighted) exchange rates of each of the regional francs should move by similar amount. If each region's franc floated freely, equiproportionate change in their trade weighted values would be accomplished by the Alsatian franc falling least against the Deutsche mark, followed closely by the Lorraine franc: the Bordeaux franc would score among the largest changes against the Deutsche mark. In sum, the correlation of rates of change of the dollar exchange rate of eastern region francs with the mark-dollar rate would be greater than for western region francs. Eastern French provinces and Rhenish Germany would form a sub-zone within the continental European zone.

In practice, regional currencies are not found within the French state. Yet regional *real* trade-weighted exchange rates must still move equiproportionately when imbalance in French external payments is not attributable to any one region in greater measure than its economic size would suggest. As in the Mont Blanc example, the adjusting mechanism is to be found in the disparity of regional price levels.

A greater proportion of local output in Alsace is in closest competition with German goods than is true for the interior of France. Equivalently, the proportion of internationally tradable output in Alsace is higher: that property is due to the differing transport costs of serving domestic and foreign markets. The transport costs of shipping goods from West Germany to Strasbourg and conversely is less than from Bordeaux. Local regional products in competition with German would be linked closely in price. A larger share of goods on display in a Strasbourg than a Bordeaux supermarket are likely to be of German origin. Thus the impact effect of a Deutsche mark-French franc appreciation on both the regional consumer price index and the ratio of the composite price index of exportable goods (internationally and to other French regions) to non-tradable goods is higher in Alsace than in the French interior. In consequence the incentive to reduce imports and increase exports is there the greatest: the impact of the franc-mark exchange rate change is greater on the external payments of Alsace than any other region.

In the longer term, the grown Alsatian surplus must be brought back into balance with the rest of France. That is accomplished by the classical adjustment mechanism of a fixed exchange rate system. Increased expenditure by local residents is induced by the build up of money balances in Alsace, which are fuelled by the trade imbalance. Increased expenditure causes the price of goods which are not traded inter-regionally or internationally to rise faster in Alsace than elsewhere. Eventually the composite price index of inter-regionally and internationally tradable goods in Alsace must be brought back to the same proportion of the local index of non-traded goods as in the other regions of France. Consistently the consumer price index of all goods will have risen more in Alsace than in other regions.

Benelux countries are in a similar in-between position to their two large neighbours, France and Germany, as is Alsace. Their political independence, however, enables them to issue an independent money. The advantages for them of floating their own currency can be deduced from the Alsatian example. A freely floating Benelux currency would tend to rise against the French franc when the Deutsche mark did, but by less. A higher proportion of Benelux than of French trade is with West Germany, and if the payments imbalance of the latter does not have a disproportionate counterpart in Benelux payments, the trade-weighted Benelux exchange rate should not be differentially affected from the French one.

The differential motion of the Benelux currency from its two large neighbours eliminates the danger that external payments equilibrium will have to be achieved by the more painful mechanism of the consumer price level rising at a different rate from that in the country with which it forms a currency bloc. The mechanism is painful because it involves an excessive growth of traded goods production, which must eventually be reversed.

Natural ties?

A parable of Ferdinando Martini, 'Animali Musicisti,' (*Opere*, Ed. Garzanti, Milan, 1873) describes how a bear, an ass, a monkey and a zebra decided to form a quartet with the idea of touring the world to earn money. They practised for many weeks under some lime trees, but things did not go well. Then the bear suggested that they practised sitting down instead of standing up. Again their performance did not improve. Then suddenly they heard a nightingale singing above them. The monkey said to the nightingale, 'you are a great artist, advice us how to become so!' and the nightingale replied 'you are not born musicians, and neither standing, nor sitting, not even if you practised for one hundred years, would you perform like me.'

In the world of currencies, some by their geographic position are naturally tied to either the Deutsche mark or the US dollar, and their motion will be closely related. However assiduously a central bank of one of Germany's small neighbours tried to make its currency behave as if in the dollar zone, it would be thwarted continuously. The Canadian dollar, by contrast, would float along with the US dollar without any direction from the Bank of Canada.

2 Money Polytheism

International investors divide into different currency creeds. First, there are the money *monotheists*, who use one reference currency for measuring their wealth and its growth over time. Monotheists 'dream' in a currency whose volatility in real purchasing power is believed to be small. The money *polytheists* are not content to use only one reference money, realizing that each has potential weaknesses as an ultimate standard of value. They measure their wealth, and investment calculations, against a basket composed of two or more monies in constant proportion to each other. The money *agnostics* reject the use of a standard composed of currencies in fixed weights. They are searching constantly to assess the 'real' purchasing power of their wealth and its optimal investment measured in terms of consumer purchasing power now and in the future. The agnostics must redetermine incessantly the currency mix of their standard by questioning the fundamental qualities – the hardness or softness – of each component money.

In the 1970s a new doctrine filtered into currency investment art. Its origin was the 'efficient market theory' which had been popularized first in the analysis of US equity markets. There, the theory stated that the present price of a security discounted the sum of knowledge about its anticipated future returns. The 'outside' investor could not hope to profit from fundamental type research: he was best to buy simply a portfolio of equities, well diversified, and mix it with a holding of risk free securities – meaning US Treasury Bills. The exact mix would be determined by each individual's attitude towards risk. This 'nihilist' theory has in recent years been extended to currency investment. It is argued that the currency investor should hold simply a portfolio of foreign currencies weighted in proportion to their net supply to non-residents of the issuing country together with his domestic currency which is assumed to be riskless. The division of his wealth between the foreign currency portfolio and his domestic money is again determined by individual risk preference.

A major flaw of the 'nihilist' theory of currency investment is its identification typically of the domestic currency as riskless. In reality, the international investor must himself search for the mix of currencies which he regards as riskless (or almost riskless). An Argentine investor will not consider the peso as low risk, so high and volatile is the peso rate of inflation. A Luxembourg investor will almost certainly not identify a 100 per cent holding of Luxembourg francs as riskless. So much of his consumption is devoted to foreign goods that his portfolio risk would be reduced by holding foreign currencies.

Applications of the efficient market theory and its 'nihilist' currency market counterparts ignore often the importance of transaction costs. Failure to recognise explicitly costs of transferring financial assets is analogous to omitting consideration of friction in the physical sciences.

In this chapter, the individual's search for the low risk currency mix and the minimization of transaction costs are demonstrated as the twin basic themes of currency analysis. Efficient market doctrine, carefully interpreted, has not swept away the artists of currency portfolio construction. Before proceeding to describe the remaining concerns of currency analysis, some applications of efficient market theory are presented.

EXCHANGE RATE FORECASTING

The economic forecaster should be concerned foremost with predicting such items as GNP, the consumer price index, industrial production, the trade balance, unemployment, and other such macro-variables. He is on much more treacherous ground when forecasting interest rates, exchange rates, the price of gold and silver, the level of the Wall Street index, or the price of an IBM share.

The forecaster blazes the trail for speculators in money and commodity markets by predicting the time-path of variables which cannot themselves be much influenced by speculation. Such variables shall be termed here as 'non-speculative.'

The expected time-path of a non-speculative variable does not affect its present level which is determinable at any date from past history. The forecaster of non-speculative variables can use as input, data observed almost entirely from the present and previous periods.

Speculative variables are forward-looking. A change in the expected time-path of the price of gold will impact immediately on the present price, which is a barometer of market expectations concerning net demand for the metal in future periods. The spot price of the Deutsche mark in terms of dollars is determined by speculators' expectations of the price in future periods: these expectations are formed from projecting the net demand for marks in the present and future periods on the basis of balance of payments forecasts. Balance of payments accounts should be broken into speculative and non-speculative variable components. Current account balances are determined in general non-speculatively and depend mainly on previous history. Exceptionally, current accounts can be speculatively influenced, as during a currency crisis, when inventories of imported goods may be built up. Capital accounts are determined almost entirely speculatively: most capital flows involve investment decisions, which are forward-looking. It is possible, though, to categorize countries as either long-term exporters or importers of capital, and long-term capital movements can so be in part inferred from past habit.

The currency speculator should utilize in his appraisal an econometric model of current account determination. He should use as inputs into his model the present effective (trade-weighted) exchange rate, and forward effective rates. The latter can be calculated as weighted averages of forward exchange rates. Forward rates are often not obtainable beyond one year ahead: they should then be imputed from bond yield differentials.

The model, having been fed with the data described, should then churn out current account forecasts for each period ahead. To these current account figures are added the estimate of long term capital flows, to arrive at a *basic payments balance* in each period. The speculator chooses a horizon date by which he hopes to have closed his position. Suppose that horizon is six months ahead. The speculator must ask whether the six-month forward exchange rates are good estimators of what the spot rates will be in six months, given that his current account forecast for the beyond is then unchanged. If his basic balance forecasts are equal to the average of those of other speculators, he should find that they tend towards zero, and he should not contest the forward exchange rate as a predictor of the spot rate. If, instead, his forecasts suggest continuing large basic imbalance, with little trend towards improvement, they are at odds with the 'average.' He should try to ascertain in which period his forecasts begin to differ markedly from those obtained by most other speculators. He would choose a horizon date in that period, believing, that actual statistics will prove his forecast to be nearer the truth, and that others in the market will trim their forecasts to figures nearer his own. The adjustment of the spot and forward exchange rates at that time will provide his speculative profit.

His speculative profit cannot be estimated econometrically. Although his chances of earning speculative profit by the horizon date are increased by his forecast being nearer than the average to basic balance data published in the intervening period, two main uncertainties prevent precise estimation of his expected profit.

First, he cannot foretell how the market will react to its average forecast having proved wrong. Will all future forecasts then be revised to be consistent with those of the model used by our speculator? Or will the present error be merely a ripple on the mill pond of near-term forecasts, without further influence? In the second type of market reaction, the discrepancy between spot and forward exchange rates at the horizon date and those imputed in the forward rate structure at the initial date will be less than in the first type. Speculative profit will be less.

Second, there is the immeasurability of the glacier named 'NET INVESTOR OVERHANG', which is the source of one tributary entering the mainstream of 'SHORT-TERM CAPITAL FLOWS.' 'NET INVESTOR OVERHANG' for dollars equals in size the excess of low-risk portfolio demand for dollar investments over the low-risk borrowing demand for dollars. Low-risk demand and supply of a currency is that arising out of the structuring of liabilities and assets that form part of the low-risk component of the international investor's portfolio.

In long-run equilibrium, 'NET INVESTOR OVERHANG' must have melted away to nothing. Melting occurs under the sustained heat of speculative activity. Until then, 'NET INVESTOR OVERHANG' consists in the total of dollars short-sold by speculators to long-run investors. Speculators short-sell dollars when the exchange rate has risen sufficiently, under the impact of net investment demand, for them to believe that the resulting deterioration in the basic balance of payments of the issuing country will cause a rapid enough return of the exchange rate to its initial real level to provide a tempting rate of profit. Residents of the country of issue borrow to pay for imports of goods and securities in excess of exports, and one source of finance is the glacier, which melts as speculators close their short positions in dollars.

The currency speculator should, in principle, estimate the rate of capital inflow from the glacier 'NET INVESTMENT OVERHANG', and include it as a component of an adjusted basic balance of payments forecast. In practice the rate of flow is submerged under 'short-term capital flows' in balance of payments statistics. Such statistics include only a global measure of short and long-term capital flows, of which the glacier is but one source. Thus, for years ahead the speculator might forecast a steady flow of short-term capital inflow from the glacier and yet he cannot hope that published balance of payments statistics will persuade others to revise their forecasts of the steady inflow of capital into line with his own, at which time the exchange rate would adjust to provide his profit. The speculator can hope thus to gain little from trying to improve on the average forecast of the rate of flow from the glacier. If the market believes that $200 m per annum of short-term capital inflows are in reality basic and represent the steady closing of speculative short positions, there is little to gain from arguing with that conventional wisdom.

In the unknown can originate fear and panic. Neither the size of 'NET INVESTOR OVERHANG' nor its rate of melting can be measured, and the unknown can change in size over time. The speculator must be aware of the limited area of the currency world that can be charted. Surrounding current account flows are glaciers and mountains of unknown dimension. If the market finds reason to alter its estimate of the size of the glaciers – either as reassessment or because of actual growth – the impact on exchange rates could far exceed that of a revision of current account forecasts. The speculator who stakes his judgement on his superior interpretation of economic relationships must still be full of humility.

Storable and non-storable

In general, the spot price of commodities which can be stored at low cost and of which there are abundant inventories, are most subject to forward-looking influences. Speculators can trade almost as cheaply in the spot gold or silver market as in the respective forward markets. The spot gold and silver prices are therefore particularly sensitive to expectations about future supply and demand conditions. In contrast, speculation is sometimes expensive in soft commodities such as sugar and cocoa. When inventories are low, only traders deriving convenience yield can justify holding these commodities, and speculative influences are at a low ebb in the spot market. The spot price then becomes more readily forecastable without having to consider demand and supply conditions for many periods beyond the forecasting range.

Most consumer-type goods are expensive to store, and their rate of obsolescence high. Speculative foresight plays little role in the determination of the price of furniture, washing machines, or clothes, for example. The consumer price index thus includes mostly non-speculative prices, and is a suitable subject for econometric forecasting.

Seasonality

Speculative prices can follow seasonal patterns without super-normal profit being available. Consider a freely tradable currency (pesos) of a small country (Island) whose major export revenue comes from summer tourism. Island will enjoy a large current account surplus during the summer months, but will run a sizeable deficit during the winter months. We could observe a pattern of the spot exchange rate rising from February to August, and falling from August to February. Speculators in the forward market would anticipate the cyclical movement in the spot, and the three-month forward rate would peak in May, reaching its low point in November. Covered arbitrage operations would then ensure that the three-month local interest rate peaked during the summer and reached its low point during the winter. The cyclical pattern of interest rates would prevent speculative profit being derived from the seasonal pattern of spot exchange rates. The domestic inflation rate could follow a seasonal pattern like the exchange rate: inflation would peak during the period when the exchange rate was expected seasonally to depreciate most.

The seasonal fluctuation of interest rates, and hence of forward and spot exchange rates, would be dampened by consumer arbitrage through time. Domestic consumers would try to bunch their purchases in the winter, when interest on saving was least, and accentuate saving during the summer when the short-term interest rate was highest. In turn, domestic enterprises would reduce consumer good inventories, and hence their demand for credit, during the summer. The scope for consumer arbitrage is limited by the lack of flexibility in timing regarding most consumer type purchases, and the non-storability of many consumer goods – for example, food, house accommodation, and transport.

MUSHROOMING TRANSACTION COSTS

Proliferating mushrooms are images of decay and corruption. In Ionesco's play, 'Amédée, ou Comment s'en débarrasser' (Amédée, or How to get rid of it), Amédée and his wife live cut off from the world. A shadow is cast over their marriage by the presence in the next room of a corpse. As the play proceeds, the corpse grows, at a faster and faster rate, and mushrooms proliferate in the apartment. Eventually, the door of the adjoining room bursts open. . . .

In more gloomy mood, the investor of the late 1970s may have pointed to the sprouting up of luxury bank buildings and proliferation of financial centres round the world as the symbolic mushrooms of Western economic decay. In more fanciful mood, a future state of affairs could be imagined in which the transactions industry grew at an increasingly rapid rate, encompassing an ever greater area in each city, smothering other activity in its path. That fantasy would be based on the fear that the real interest rate on investment had become very low, or even negative. Yet transaction costs had increased possibly even in real terms. Thus the industrial and commercial capital stock would be worn down gradually, as a succession of transactions would provide an opportunity for the transactions industry to chip into it: the chipping would occur at a greater rate than new investment, given the low expected real rate of return obtainable.

In this section, the threat of mushrooming transaction costs and their containment are considered. First, the growth of transaction costs in the world of floating exchange rates and high inflation rates is assessed. Second, the role of the financial instrument designer in reducing transaction costs is demonstrated. Third, the mushrooming of tax free bank intermediaries is described, and how to reduce the costs of dealing with them.

Are transaction costs growing?

A frequent grassroots business objection to floating exchange rates has been that they have caused the costs of effecting exchange transactions to increase. Yet the increased bid-offer spreads (transaction costs) in exchange markets do not necessarily mean supernormal profits for the banks. Floating exchange rates have increased the risks of their market-making activities. The volatility of exchange rates and hence the risk of inventory holding have increased for the market-maker.

Still, some sceptics may argue that the risk of inventory holding has not changed greatly since the days of fixed exchange rates. True, the volatility of exchange rates has increased: but on average, over time, banks should gain on the swings what they lose on the roundabouts. Such an argument fails to recognize the market-maker's function of maintaining a continuous quote, and so inevitably 'leaning against the wind.' If a wind of dollar short-selling to buy Deutsche marks gathers force, bank market-makers (whose function it is to maintain a continuous quote) will find that they are building up dollar inventories. Market-makers find that they build up inventories of a currency which is being increasingly speculatively short-sold, and run short of currencies being increasingly speculatively purchased. To protect themselves against loss from leaning against gathering speculative winds, bank market-makers must charge a bid-offer spread. Maintaining a continuous quote implies that the market-maker states a buying and selling price, even when in ignorance about whether a speculative flurry is transitory or heralds a speculative wind.

The increase in exchange transactions costs that has accompanied floating currencies is cause for all transactors to devote greater attention to prospective price movements. The higher are transaction costs, the less likely is it that all available information about future price trends is discounted in the present price. Such market efficiency depends on the operation of a core of well-informed speculators, ready to switch between currencies when interest rate differentials are inconsistent with their exchange rate expectations. However, the certainty of transaction costs incurred by switching can hold back pure speculative action when perceived inefficiency is not considerably greater. A commercial or investor transactor, who must make payment in a foreign currency within a fixed time limit (say, seven days), cannot avoid incurring transaction costs. He is in a different position from the pure speculator who must decide whether his game of chance is worth the certain fee charged. The commercial or investor transactor should realize that market prices with which he is confronted can be inefficient within a band whose width is determined by the pure speculator's unwillingness to incur transaction costs. It is not therefore appropriate for the investor/businessman to rest content that he need not study the market prospects because anything that he can find out will already have long since been discounted in the market price.

The significance of the *band of inefficiency* that can surround a market price increases with the size of transaction costs found there. Consider for example, the relation of one-year euro-Deutsche mark rates to one-year euro-Swiss franc interest rates. The transaction cost of switching between the two types of deposit (breaking one deposit and investing in the other) will be equal in normal market conditions to $\frac{3}{8}$ per cent in present value. The transaction cost is calculated as the sum of half the bid-offer spread in one-year euro-Deutsche marks added to half the bid-offer spread in one year euro-francs, plus exchange transaction costs, plus brokerage costs, all expressed in present value terms. A $\frac{3}{8}$ per cent deadweight cost incurred now is large, relative to the prospective expected real rate of return on money market investments (about $\frac{1}{2}$ to 1 per cent per annum on US dollars, for example, from the US resident's viewpoint). The investor who is considering whether to place money in a one-year Deutsche mark or one-year Swiss franc deposit should realize that the existence of transactions costs means that efficient speculation does not prevent the expected real return differential being nearly $\frac{1}{2}$ per cent per annum. It may therefore be profitable for the outside investor with fresh funds to research market conditions, and not assume that market prices already reflect all present knowledge.

The band of inefficiency that makes it worthwhile for the outside investor to form his own speculative judgement, is analogous to the band within which money market two-way arbitrage is not profitable for outside transactors. Suppose for example that euro-guilder (bid) rates rise above covered parity with euro-Deutsche mark (bid) rates by 3/16 per cent: that is less than the transaction costs that the non-market-maker arbitrageur will incur in borrowing euro-marks, swapping them for guilders, and investing in guilders. In time, risk arbitrage by market-makers and investor arbitrage by investors, deciding whether to invest in marks direct or in covered guilders, will narrow the differential to zero. In the meantime, profit can be earned by the investor studying the respective returns from direct and indirect investment in Deutsche marks. He should not assume that professional arbitrage, any more than professional speculation, can occur instantaneously.

Stale bull liquidation

We all know that there are many more cows than bulls. But how many of us have met stale bulls? In reality their roaming ground is confined to the commodity and currency pages of the financial press. Stale bull liquidation is reported, in the copper market for example, when a considerable number of disappointed bulls decide to close their long positions in the metal.

More generally, the suggestion that technical analysis of markets in terms of, for example, the amount of stale bull liquidation, stop loss buying and selling, provides help towards interpreting short term price movements, is evidence of the significance of the 'band of inefficiency' in speculative markets. Even if all relevant knowledge was widely shared, the market price can vary within a range equal in size to the difference between the transaction costs of cash entrants to the market and those who must first sell another investment. Persistent selling (or buying) would push the bid (or offer) price to the edge of the 'band of inefficiency', in addition to causing the band itself to move down. Not only must speculators be tempted in who are merely switching from cash, but some must be tempted who are holding less liquid assets, for which the cost of disposal is greater. Technical terms, such as 'stale bull liquidation' are suggestive of a notable shift in the composition of the speculative population. Such shifts provoke often a movement of either the bid or offer price to an edge of the band of inefficiency. Supernormal expected profits are available at such times, for those new speculators replacing the old whose transaction costs of entry are intra-marginal: it also becomes opportune for less liquid speculators to consider entry.

Switzerland, where much ends up

Scott-Fitzgerald in 'Tender is the Night' (Penguin, 1939) described Switzerland as a country 'where lots ends up, but nothing starts.' Swiss bank activities have mushroomed in the 1970s. International investment, using the vehicle of the Swiss bank account with its quality of secrecy, was spurred by severe deterioration in inflation performance of some monies, growing fears of political instability, and failure of national taxation structures to be indexed.

Although the Swiss bank account may be an essential vehicle in the flight from archaic or penal tax structures, it is not the gateway to a financial Garden of Eden, where man has no financial care. Though such thoughts might occur on a sunny day on Lake Zurich, the investor should be cautioned by the magnificence of the bank buildings which he sees. His resolve should be strengthened not to make an undue contribution to their institutional upkeep. Swiss bankers live on transaction costs charged to clients who have entered their gates; and Switzerland has become the highest income per capita country in the West, on the strength of its banking industry.

The private client of the Swiss bank cannot avoid granting some discretion to his banker. Discretion can vary from giving him power to select investments by currency and name, to power to effect routine transactions. The latter include effecting currency bond purchases and sales, as instructed by the client. He must hope that the best market rate is obtained: difficulties of communication make it impossible for the client to shop around for the best terms on every transaction. The scope for the banker to score at the expense of his discretionary client is great. The client does not have as protection – as in some centres such as Paris, Frankfurt – an official bourse fixing price at which he can insist that his transactions are effected (see chapter 5, p. 111).

More generally, the large Swiss bank should gain from being able to internalize a section of the foreign exchange market within its doors. At the beginning of each day the private client department of a Swiss bank knows that certain foreign exchange transactions are to be effected: so many Deutsche mark coupons are to be clipped and sold for Swiss francs, so many Deutsche marks are to be purchased to effect instructed euro-Deutsche mark bond purchases. The investment manager can so arrive at a net purchase (or sale) figure for each currency and transact with his foreign exchange dealer. What price does the investment manager then charge out to his 'matched' private clients? At one extreme, he would charge matched buyers and sellers the same price, equal to the average of the 'bid' and 'offer' price, making no profit on the exchange transactions: at the other extreme, he would charge the matched clients with a different price, separated by the dealer's bid-offer spread. Which method is chosen varies from bank to bank and is hidden in the Swiss banking mystique.

The Swiss 'matching' example reveals an important principle of transaction cost minimization. When a bank client reveals his intended transaction in advance, he should hope to obtain keener terms than when he demands an instantaneous quote. Advance warning provides a chance for the banker to match the order with others of which early notice is given. No dealer inventory is therefore at risk, but the client must trust that his banker will obtain the best quote. Again, to protect his position the client can instruct his banker to complete his order only on the floor of the Bourse, at fixing time. Then he has a published reference price to compare with that obtained for himself: yet he should gain from the banker being able to match his order against others he has received in the opposite direction.

Transaction costs of using the Swiss banking system do not begin and end in the investment department. A high proportion of investment funds flowing in and out of Switzerland pass through the banknote, or travellers cheque markets. In Switzerland is found the world's most active banknote market, and many investors must bring their notes there to change. Further a banknote or travellers cheque transaction is again often unavoidable if the investor wishes to utilize Swiss funds for consumption in his own country.

In short, the investor must have a positive strategy of transaction cost minimization, if his search for Swiss security is not to prove costly. At worst, he would pay a banknote, plus foreign exchange plus euro-bond transaction cost amounting to over two per cent just to set up his euro-bond portfolio.

It has been variously estimated that under the streets of Basel is found more gold than is stored at Fort Knox. The passion of Swiss account

investors for gold is not attributable simply to their search for a political
risk free asset. But long experience has taught many generations of
investors in Switzerland that gold is the least transaction cost prone asset.
Once bought and stored in the vaults, there is no further rollover
transaction cost as with fixed term bond and deposit investment. There is
an annual safekeeping fee: but the per unit value cost of upkeep of the
bank troglodyte department is less than that of the private client
investment department. Further, the dangers of discretionary management are avoided.

Financial instrument design

We do not observe today automobiles which are square in shape, nor do
we observe aeroplanes with square noses. The scientist has discovered
that streamlining reduces air friction and transport costs. Analogously,
in the securities markets very short-term bonds are not issued and small
banks do not issue certificates of deposits. The existence of the present
range and maturity of financial instruments is not random. The financial
engineer designs instruments which he believes will reduce the deadweight cost of transactions.

The two main determinants of the size of transaction costs of dealing
in a particular instrument are *first* the rate of turnover relative to
inventory that the market-makers are likely to experience and second
the price volatility of the instrument. The higher is the ratio of turnover
to inventory, and the lower the unit risk, the lower will be bid-offer
spreads. The successful designer must create an instrument in which
there will be sufficient turnover for the market-maker's spread, when
amortised over the marginal investor's expected holding period, to be
not greater than on other similar risk investments: nor must the
amortised spread over the marginal borrower's expected period of
indebtedness be greater than on other similar risk borrowing. For
simplicity, in present discussion no distinction is made between new
issue and secondary markets: the two are assumed integrated, as is in
practice true for the bank deposit market.

The instrument designer faces a trade-off between maturity and
turnover. The shorter the maturity, the higher is the rate of turnover: the
body of investors who hold till maturity will have to roll over the
instrument more often. As illustration, the bid-offer spreads (in terms of
purchase price) on one to twelve-month deposits grow approximately in
proportion with maturity. Yet risk (volatility) of the present value of
deposits grows at a declining rate with maturity. The pattern of bid-offer

spreads is explained by a declining turnover rate with maturity which just counters the influence of the less-than-proportionate increase in risk.

The individual investor himself faces a trade-off between transaction costs and his intended holding period. The longer he can hold a security, without being obliged to realize it, the lower should be his rate of incurring transaction cost. If his intended holding period is, say three months, he should find that the amortised transaction cost of buying a three month deposit is less than rolling over one month deposits, even though the transaction cost per unit turnover is least on the latter. Disparity in intended holding periods helps to explain the range of maturities found. Conceptually, we may range investment funds in a ladder, each step having different intended holding periods.

In most money and bond markets, a 'gap' exists between the money market up to twelve months maturity, and the bond market with maturities of four years and beyond. Old or stale bonds of less than four years maturity exist, but they are little traded, and new issues are not generally made in that range. A possible explanation is that investment funds looking for one to four years average holding period are insufficient to provide a turnover rate relative to inventory risk that will allow market-makers to quote profitably a bid-offer spread low enough for its amortised cost to be less than on rolling over one-year deposits.

The yield curve in money and bond markets has long been an area studied by economists. The 'natural habitat' theory has postulated that investors (and borrowers) are segmented by their preferred maturities. Insurance companies for example wish to invest long, banks to invest short. Such preferred habitats imply that yield differentials between short and long instruments can differ by more than expectations of short-term interest rate movements, and include also a risk premium.

The present discussion has sidestepped the mainstream literature, which has tended to ignore the question of how transaction costs vary with maturity. The purpose has been here to show that the maturity structure of transaction costs, combined with natural habitats – or ranges of preferred maturities – can explain the age structure of instruments available in bond and money markets.

Age reduces investment appeal

Bonds lose their appeal to new investors in their old age, and become more closely attached to their present holders. Market-making spreads are much greater in euro-bonds of one-year maturity than in one year bank deposits or certificates of deposit. In the dollar denominated sector of the euro-markets, bid-offer spreads in one-year bonds are around $\frac{1}{2}$ per cent, whilst in one-year deposits are around $\frac{1}{8}$ per cent. The higher spread is due to a lower turnover rate of bond than deposit inventories. Whilst banks issue continuously deposits, and are market-makers in bank deposits, corporations are not typically market-makers in their own debts, and these are issued usually under a type of auction arrangement. Further, corporations incur fixed costs in issuing bond instruments in the open market, and they will find it more expensive to issue one-year bonds than borrow from a bank which in turn issues one-year deposits. The stock of bonds with lives of one year and less is not supplied by new issues which would contribute to turnover and so to lower spreads. Rather it is supplied by the ageing of longer bonds, as they approach redemption. The metamorphosis of ageing does not require trading.

Some designers of bonds have tried to use turnover stimulants with the hope of boosting the liquidity of their instrument. In the floating rate sector, for example, minimum rate provisions are common. In the domestic US corporate bond market, bonds are frequently issued with a 'sweetener' in the form of a stock warrant. Both additions, in floating and fixed rate markets respectively, attract speculative interest. Speculators are more active traders than investors seeking a low risk store of value. Persistent speculative turnover should contribute towards a lowering of bid-offer spreads.

Designing certificates of deposit

Transaction cost considerations help explain why negotiable certificates of deposit in the euro-dollar markets are issued only by large banks. Even in their deposit business, small banks are likely to suffer from a low rate of turnover relative to inventory. Their bid-offer spread quoted on deposit or loan interbank business will usually be wider than for large banks. Two considerations enable them to compete for non-bank deposit and loan business, despite their comparative disadvantage in the pure market-making function. *First*, they may have particular relationships – based presumably on special knowledge about their customers, or expertise – which are responsible for a steady flow of non-bank deposit and loan business. The relationship with a borrower may enable him to obtain cheaper terms despite the small bank's market-making disadvantage: depositors may accept a slightly less competitive quote, given other attractive services that are being offered. *Second*, the bank knows the dates on which its regular clients are likely to rollover their loans and deposits. Similar to practice in the foreign exchange market, advance knowledge of transactions provides scope for 'netting' the amount of business that must be offset in the market, and dealing costs per transaction should be reduced.

The two considerations above, which enable small banks to compete successfully with large ones in taking deposits from and making loans to non-bank customers, are not relevant to the certificate of deposit market. Such certificates are bearer – the identity of the holder being unknown to the issuer. Timing of purchases and sales in the secondary market is unpredictable. The low volume of turnover in the small bank CDs would cause the bid-offer spreads in such instruments to be wider than for large bank CDs. They would thus be difficult to issue, except at rates significantly higher than large bank CDs, and probably almost equal to the quoted deposit rate. There is the further danger that the offer rate on small bank CDs in the secondary market could sometimes – given its narrowness – rise above the rate at which the bank would have expected to be able to raise inter-bank finance, and that source would be jettisoned. Why should other banks lend it money direct, when a better rate is obtainable from buying its CDs which are temporarily in excess supply? Outstanding CDs could therefore threaten the small bank's programming of financing differences between known deposit and loan rollovers, and advance programming must be adopted to remain competitive.

IN SEARCH OF A STANDARD

In *Money, Hard and Soft*, I described how international investors tend to select a 'dream money' – normally Swiss francs, Deutsche marks, or US dollars, – in which to measure their portfolio, and hence in which to denominate a high proportion of their international monetary liabilities and assets. The purpose here is to identify the considerations which are relevant to the choice of a dream money, and when the investor should dream in more than one money. In the terminology of the present chapter, a currency monotheist dreams in one money: the currency polytheist dreams in many. In more mundane language, how does each individual select what is for him the lowest risk asset?

Climate influences currency choice

Not all investors have to make a positive choice of currency standard.

Residents of Chicago, Dusseldorf, or Zurich, are all based in the hinterlands of countries which issue freely tradable international monies. It may still be arguable that even the inhabitants of those three cities could be accused of 'own money illusion' if they consider the local money, undiluted with others, to be their lowest risk asset. Restless souls would search for other additions to the local money for the low risk component of their portfolio, particularly those in Zurich and Dusseldorf.

Many international investors come from harsher monetary environments than the three described. Latin Americans, Italians, and Frenchmen, to name only a few, live in countries whose local monies are not freely tradable, can be subject to high rates of inflation, and are politically risky. Prudent investors in those countries hold monetary portfolios externally, and they must select among available international monies one or a combination of several which will make up their low risk portfolio.

Risk is defined in relation to real purchasing power. The risk of an international money is perceived differently according to where the investor intends to spend his wealth, and at what date he intends to spend it. The resident of a country which is part of a polar field will generally find that the pole currency is the lowest risk international money over short periods in terms of his consumer purchasing power. Thus, so closely correlated are short term changes in the French franc-dollar and Deutsche mark-dollar, especially during periods of transzonal payments crises, that the Deutsche mark will be the lowest risk international money for short periods from the viewpoint of the Frenchman.

Risk of an international money can be divided conceptually into two components, real external risk, and real internal risk. Real external risk measures the volatility of the investor's real purchasing power caused by fluctuations in the real exchange rate between the international money and his own local one. Real internal risk measures the volatility of the investor's real purchasing power caused by fluctuations in the domestic rate of inflation in the country of issue of the international money.

Real external risk is a lower proportion of real exchange rate volatility for a large currency such as the dollar than of a small currency such as the Swiss franc. The US accounts for the largest share of world trade, and a considerable proportion of world trade is denominated in dollars. Further, a dollar depreciation raises the dollar price level of internationally traded goods to a lesser extent than a smaller currency

(Swiss franc) depreciation would raise the Swiss franc price level of internationally traded goods, at least in the short and medium term. US and dollar zone purchasing power is of considerably greater importance than Swiss purchasing power in most world commodity markets whereby demand measured in dollars is less sensitive than demand measured in francs to changes in the franc-dollar exchange rate.

The US economy's large size bestows a unique advantage on the US dollar as a competitor of other international monies. Suppose that the volatility of six-month changes in the nominal French franc-dollar and French franc-Deutsche mark exchange rates were the same. Then, from the viewpoint of a Frenchman, the six-monthly volatility of real purchasing power of marks should be greater than of dollars. That follows from the volatility of the dollar price of internationally traded goods being less than the mark one, whereas the strong zonal association of the franc and mark found for monthly intervals weakens for longer time changes. The dollar would tend so to be favoured in medium term portfolios.

In portfolios designed for consumption in the longer term, real internal price risk is of much greater concern for the choice of low risk money than is real external price risk. The size of real external price risk is limited: many studies have shown that real exchange rates fluctuate within a band which rarely exceeds 20 per cent from par. In contrast, there is no limit to cumulative differential movement of price levels internationally: their difference can grow geometrically over time. Whereas real exchange rates fluctuate more than inflation rate differentials in the short term, over long periods the converse is true. Thus, the Swiss franc gains favour relative to dollars in long-term portfolios. Although the short-term real external risk of the Swiss franc is greater than of the dollar for residents of almost all countries other than Switzerland, the long term real internal risk of the Swiss franc is believed to be considerably less than of the dollar. Over the next ten years, the investor may consider the likely range of inflation in the USA and Switzerland to be 5–15 per cent and 0–4 per cent respectively: further he considers the maximum real exchange rate fluctuation of the franc over the 10 year period from base value to be 30 per cent. Then the Swiss franc would be a lower risk long-term asset (or liability) than the dollar, if designed in fixed interest rate form. Where the interest rate on the long-term instrument is free to fluctuate with market rates and hence inflation expectations – or equivalently, if the investor intends to roll-over short-term instruments – the particular attraction of the Swiss franc is reduced. The development of a large market in floating rate notes in euro-dollars during the late 1970s should have reduced the significance of inflation volatility as a determinant of portfolio choice.

Wealthy investors tend to have a longer term horizon than smaller ones. Their rate of consumption relative to present worth is less. In consequence, the Swiss franc should be especially popular in large portfolios, the dollar should be popular in medium portfolios, and the regional polar currency should be most popular in very short-term or small portfolios.

The construction of the low-risk portfolio is an art-form. The different weightings given each international money depends on the time horizon of the investor, and on his country of residence. Further, the risk relations which are the basis of his judged weightings can change. Perceived inflation volatilities and exchange rate correlations fluctuate, sometimes dramatically, as at times of international monetary disorder. So complex an art can low risk portfolio construction become, that the currency monotheists believe in choosing simply one money as their standard, and sticking to it.

Manufactured currency hybrids

In the mid-1970s, currency hybrids were briefly fashionable as denominators in the international money and bond markets. EUAs (European Units of Account) and SDRs (Special Drawing Rights) were the principal denominators. These hybrids were baskets of currencies, weighted in fixed proportion. Such hybrids are fast becoming candidates for inclusion in a museum of international monetary history, just as pre-Napoleonic shoes are now a curiosum in clothes museums. Pre-Napoleonic shoe makers failed to realize that shoes should be designed differently for left and right feet. Hybrid money instrument designers must realize that investors with varying geographical location and consumption horizons desire very different weightings in their low risk currency portfolio.

In retrospect, the attempt to popularize currency hybrids was doomed to failure. The hybrids all included as components some monies that were not internationally popular. The components of the EUA and SDR are shown in figure 2.1. Both the EUA and SDR exclude the Swiss franc, an obvious candidate for the international portfolio.

At best, the manufacturers of hybrids could have marketed their product by demonstrating their potential to reduce the transaction costs of currency diversification, especially for the smaller investor. The appeal of currency hybrids would have been similar to that of unit trusts

1 EUA = Dm 0.828 + Ffr 1.15 + £ 0.0885
        + Lit 109 + D.fl 0.286 + Bfr 3.66
        + Dkr 0.217 + £ IR 0.00759
        + Lux fr. 0.14

1 SDR = $ 0.40 + Dm 0.38 + £ 0.045
        + Ffr 0.44 + ¥ 26 + Can.$ 0.071
        + Lit 47 + Dfl 0.14 + Bfr 1.6
        + Skr 0.13 + $A 0.012 + Dkr 0.11
        + Nkr 0.099 + Pta 1.1 + Sch. 0.22
        + Rand 0.0082

Figure 2.1 Components of SDR and EUA

for small investor equity investment. If sufficient numbers of small investors had been interested in a standardized diversified currency portfolio, represented by the EUA or SDR, market-making spreads for small transactions in these could have been less than the composite spread on buying and selling each denomination of currency investment separately. Standardization is a common technique of financial instrument design and is used to develop a market for smaller transactors in which dealing costs are less than in wholesale markets. In *Money, Hard and Soft*, the standardization technique and its application was described for the Chicago International Monetary Market (see pp. 80–5).

The potential transactions cost advantage of the currency hybrids increases with the number of minor currencies in the hybrid. For example, the transactions cost saved by dealing in SDRs rather than in each component separately should be greater than that saved by dealing in a hypothetical hybrid consisting of only Deutsche marks, Swiss francs, yen, and US dollars, rather than in each currency separately. Broad exchange markets exist in the mark, franc, dollar and yen. The manufacturers of the SDR or EUA hybrids, though recognizing that their service was to reduce the transaction costs of diversification, over-estimated in what degree diversification was at all useful. Currency zone analysis suggests that diversification need extend only to polar currencies plus the currencies whose internal properties of stability are exceptional, for example the Swiss franc. If only these three or four currencies are included, then the possible advantages of hybrids, even to the smaller investor, appear highly dubious.

The discussion so far has concentrated on the private market use of hybrids. In the world of official institutions, SDRs and EUAs have become established units of account with the International Monetary Fund and EEC respectively. Political motives dictate that no one national currency could be used to denominate the transactions of a multinational official institution. Gold has similarly been ruled out by political considerations. Currency hybrids have gained acceptance as a realization of political compromise. In the private markets, where political costs and benefits are not a determining factor of monetary taste, SDRs and EUAs have proved a failure.

Gold is a Swiss franc commodity

One of the stated advantages of the dollar as a component of medium-term low-risk portfolios was that a high proportion of world trade is denominated in US dollars. Commodity futures markets, wherever situated, are almost always based on dollar prices. Where exceptions exist, such as in the London Metal Exchange, the explanation is to be found in local exchange control regulations, which inhibit residents from trading in currencies other than their own. The predominance of dollar pricing in international commodity markets is attributable in part to transaction costs in dollar foreign exchange markets being less than between non-dollar currencies (see *Money, Hard and Soft*, pp. 141–3). Hence use of dollar denomination is likely to minimize total transaction costs of all users of these markets, where users are of multifarious currency base.

The dollar's predominance as unit of account in commodity markets is based on more than its exchange transaction cost advantage: it is often the appropriate speculative numeraire to choose. The speculator in sugar futures, for example, claims his special expertise in forecasting future supply and demand conditions of sugar. His choice of currency against which to trade sugar is determined by the desire to insulate his reward for judging physical conditions correctly from exchange rate fluctuations. His problem of choice is analogous to that of the currency speculator in choosing between US dollar and Deutsche mark numeraires (see figure 1.2). Suggested speculative numeraires in commodity markets are illustrated in figure 2.2.

A 'dollar commodity' is defined here as one whose numeraire for speculative judgement should be the US dollar: A 'Swiss franc commodity' is one whose speculative numeraire should be the Swiss franc.

The statistical criterion of the optimum speculative numeraire, say shekels, is that the correlation of changes in the shekel price of the commodity in question with changes in the shekel price of the key currencies – dollars and marks – is least, where changes are measured

	US dollar	Swiss franc	British pound
copper	X		
Persian rugs	X		
tea			X
gold	where subject of speculation includes general movement of funds in or out of the US$ and effects on gold price.	where subject of speculation is specific to gold market e.g. natural supply shortages, increased jewellery demand.	

Figure 2.2 Speculative Numeraires in commodity markets

over the speculative horizon. The correlation of changes in the dollar price of copper with changes in the dollar exchange rate of the mark is presently less than that between changes in the mark price of copper and changes in the mark rate of the dollar, where time intervals correspond to those most commonly found in commodity futures markets. The explanation for the finding is the greater importance of US than West German purchasing power in the copper market.

Tea is a British pound commodity. Britain is by far the most important market for tea, and hence the demand for tea is most sensitive to fluctuations in the British pound exchange rate. Another example of a traditional British pound commodity is jute.

Gold since 1976 has behaved like a Swiss franc commodity. Monthly changes in the dollar price of gold and the Swiss franc-dollar exchange rate have been highly correlated. An abstract Swiss franc-gold zone is identifiable, with the Swiss franc sometimes being polar with respect to gold. Monthly changes in the gold-Swiss franc price are related insignificantly to monthly changes in the Swiss franc-dollar exchange rate. Hence, the Swiss franc is the appropriate numeraire for speculative positions whose motive base is knowledge about developments specific to the gold market; IMF or US Treasury auctions, jewellery demand, newly mined supply, growth in popularity relative to the Swiss franc. Where the basis of speculation is belief in the imminence of a flight from the dollar, then the dollar is the obvious speculative numeraire.

How can the close correlation between short-term change in the dollar price of gold and Swiss francs be explained? First, both are considered to be of low political risk. Hence, when political risks become prominent, both demand for gold and the Swiss franc will be affected similarly. Second, it is widely believed that the rate of increase of the Swiss monetary base, and of the physical gold stock above ground, have a naturally low ceiling. At times when scares exist about the stability of US monetary policy, both the Swiss franc and gold are favoured as hedges. Third, changes in net investment demand for the franc and gold are likely to be larger relative to structural changes in net commercial supply of francs or gold than is true for other international monies. Both the Swiss franc and gold react more to net investment outflows (or inflows) from the dollar than other principal alternatives, such as the Deutsche mark. Fourth, investor demand for gold and Swiss francs has come traditionally much more from Europe than from dollar zone countries. European zone investors tend to have a target proportion of their wealth – measured in terms of their low risk asset, or dream money – to be held in gold and Swiss francs. Thus changes in the level of dollar zone against mark zone currencies influence the dollar demand for physical gold, by the operation of a 'wealth effect'. A two-way relation exists between gold's popularity in European portfolios, and the metal's membership of a franc zone. The close correlation of the dollar price of gold with the dollar price of mark zone currencies should itself increase gold's prominence in European portfolios.

The choice of the Swiss franc as the speculative numeraire for gold depends on the further critical assumption that large fluctuations in the Swiss franc-gold price are more likely to have their basis in events specific to the gold than to the Swiss franc market. An analogy exists in the choice of the mark as speculative numeraire for the Swiss franc (see pp. 14–15). The mark's numeraire property was shown to depend on German predominance in trade. The Swiss franc's numeraire property in gold trading depends on gold, while in many respects being like an international money, still retaining some characteristics of its family of origin, i.e. the metals. During periods of metal shortage, or stockpile reductions, the gold price of Swiss francs can fluctuate widely, irrespective of the conditions in the Swiss franc market. It is difficult to imagine reversely a situation of acute shortage or excess supply of Swiss base money, composed of Swiss banknotes and deposits with the Swiss National Bank. Should gold ever become again a unit of account in international capital markets, the gold price would become less sensitive to conditions of metallic supply and demand (see *Money, Hard and Soft*, pp. 147–151). Then, the suitability of the Swiss franc as numeraire for gold speculation would have to be reassessed.

Marcel Aymé, in one of his fantasy stories, describes how two children bring a wolf home, tame him, and train him to partake in their games. One day, the children decide to play 'wolf'. The wolf, wild with excitement, cannot prevent his original nature coming to the fore . . . The parallel position of gold as a member of the set of international monies is apparent when all paper money issuers play the game of inflation or restricting convertibility: then gold can swallow up its paper contenders as the ultimate store of value.

Is the dollar numeraire secure?

The dollar's comparative advantage as a numeraire in commodity futures markets was found to depend on the large size of the US economy. Two developments could undermine the dollar numeraire; first, growing inflation volatility in the US; second, increasing correlation between the movement of West European dollar exchange rates.

If the US rate of inflation became much more volatile than the West German, then changes in the dollar price of world primary commodities (sugar, coffee, copper, for example) would become more sensitive to changes in nominal exchange rates than would changes in their mark price, despite the larger share of the USA than West Germany in world trade. A large proportion of dollar-mark exchange rate movements would be due to US inflation volatility rather than to real exchange rate volatility. Although the dollar has a head start as numeraire because of its low real external risk, high inflation volatility can more than cancel its natural advantage. Erosion of the dollar numeraire would occur first in its role as denominator of long-term contracts. For short-term contracts, real external risk would remain more important than inflation risk, except under conditions of severe double digit inflationary disease.

Increasing correlation between European dollar exchange rates could occur with or without a formal monetary agreement. Natural reasons would include increasing intra-European trade, growing dominance of the Deutsche mark, and pursuance of similar monetary policies. Explicit exchange management would be exemplified by an extension of the European Snake. Increasing correlation of European dollar exchange rates would decrease the impact of Deutsche mark-US dollar fluctuations on the mark price of world commodities since a large part of world purchasing power would be from mark related countries.

The dollar's numeraire property in world trade explains why volatility of US inflation rates is of more than domestic US concern. The volatility of price of world primary commodities, measured in dollars, is an increasing function of volatility of the US price level. As the dollar is the natural speculative numeraire for commodity trading, fine judge-ment in commodity speculation becomes less worthwhile as US inflation becomes more volatile, because rewards are more likely to be undermined by monetary or currency fluctuations.

Trading platinum against gold

So far, the search has been for the most suitable *currency* numeraire for commodity speculation and trading. Sometimes, however, speculators trade one commodity against another. A conceptual commodity geography may be derived analogously to the currency geography outlined in chapter one. Commodity zones are based not on geographic or monetary interdependence, but on interdependence in physical supply and demand. A polar commodity's power is derived from the relative size of its annual production. Thus copper, zinc, and lead form a commodity zone, with copper sometimes being polar with respect to the others.

In precious metals, gold, silver, platinum, and palladium may be identified as forming a zone. At times, gold is polar with respect to the other three, but particularly platinum. During a US dollar exchange crisis, for example, the correlation of changes in the dollar price of gold and platinum becomes particularly high, both tending to be recipients of flows of flight money in and out of the US money. At such times, a speculator wanting to take advantage of knowledge specific to the platinum market (for example, forthcoming Russian sales of the metal) would trade platinum against the gold numeraire. The small size of the platinum market suggests that changing conditions there cannot much influence the dollar price of gold.

The golden polar field is not presently large. In what circumstances could its range become extended? Consider a world in which inflation rates in every country were highly volatile, and not much correlated internationally. Then long-run changes in the gold price of a primary commodity (say, copper) may be less sensitive to long run changes in the price of gold against key currencies, than long-run dollar or mark price changes of the commodity to long-run changes of the dollar or mark against gold. Except in a world of universal hyperinflation, the gold numeraire is unlikely to penetrate short-term commodity markets. There, real exchange risk remains the dominant component of currency risk, and the money of the largest trading nation (or area) should be expected to remain as numeraire.

DOLLAR IN DECLINE?

Some scholars have claimed that the decline of the Roman empire set in when Varius's legions were defeated by the Germans in the rule of Augustus. From that date Rome never dared again to extend its frontiers East of the Rhine. But it should not be forgotten that many Romans continued to prosper until the final sacking of Rome almost four hundred years later. Monetary historians in numbers of years to come may with hindsight name that day in August 1971 when the dollar's link with gold was broken as the start of its decline as an international money. But unless the world monetary order is shaken by earthquake, a decline in the dollar's role would have to be a slow and non-continuous process.

The clue to the built-in resistances to a rapid decline in the dollar's international role is found in our previous discussion of real external and internal risk (see p. 50). Suppose real internal risk of the US dollar increases. Then investors will (on a net basis) tend to switch to other monies, notably the Deutsche mark and Swiss franc. The increasing net investor overhang for these other monies will increase the real exchange rate volatility of both the Swiss franc-US dollar and the Deutsche mark-US dollar. Market estimation of overhang is very imprecise and likely to fluctuate widely through time. The smaller size of West Germany and Switzerland means that a larger share of real exchange rate volatility of the Deutsche mark and Swiss franc is translated into real external risk than of real exchange rate volatility of the US dollar, from the viewpoint of most international investors. Thus, an essential fuse breaks too rapid a flow of funds from the dollar into the Deutsche mark and Swiss franc overhang. A perceived increase in US inflation volatility triggers a rush of funds into the mark and franc overhang and so real external risk grows faster in marks and francs than in dollars. At the margin, the briefly opened risk advantage obtained by shifting into marks and francs from dollars is soon eliminated.

No such brake-fuse would exist for investment outflows from the Swiss franc, which is the smallest of the international monies. Indeed, an outflow provoked by an increase in the franc's relative real internal risk could soon develop into a flood of ever greater size. In such a period of uncertainty about the size of continued international investor demand for francs, the volatility of the franc-dollar exchange rate would increase. The real external risk of the franc would so be increased at a faster rate than that of the dollar, from the viewpoint of most investors, further discouraging investment holdings.

Asymmetry between borrower and lender

To some extent, increased real internal risk of the dollar would encourage international borrowers, as well as investors, to switch to alternative international monies. Yet, there are reasons to suppose that the marginal propensity to switch to alternatives is greater for investors than borrowers in response to a given deterioration of the dollar's real internal risk.

Borrowers in the international markets are almost entirely institutional. Most institutions have to report their financial position at regular intervals, and a given unit of account is stipulated in their articles of association. Whereas the alert individual will respond to increased US inflation volatility by decreasing the share of the dollar in his low risk portfolio and 'dream' unit of account, the institutional treasurer is not normally free to do so.

The pre-eminence of reporting accounts in US dollars among multinational corporations, implies that the dollar will long be the favourite currency in international borrowing. Treasurers are concerned with reducing the volatility of reported dollar profits, rather than with reducing the volatility of profits measured in real purchasing power measured by weights which reflect the global spread of shareholders. If corporate treasurers became convinced of the advantages of reporting in a currency basket, or another money, many years would elapse before the lawyers had accommodated the change. The heavy hand of the Law and the predominant size of Wall Street among world equity markets would combine to slow borrowers in changing their currency preferences.

3 Alternatives to the Dollar

Blue and brown used to be combined only rarely in clothing design. Then the one thousand and second tale of the Arabian nights unfolded: one day in late 1973 the total wealth of Arabia was quadrupled. The redistribution of world purchasing power brought new influences to bear on fashion-making. Blue and brown are the colours of the desert. They are a traditional mix in oriental art, notably in Persian rugs. By 1977 the blue-and-brown combination had become popular even in Chicago, where blue and brown umbrellas were the season's rage!

Arabian influence on fashion extended beyond clothing. Investors in all countries followed the prevailing nomadic trend. Much investment and borrowing is now undertaken by corporations and individuals who have no natural or national preference for one currency rather than another. Neither accumulated OPEC surpluses nor tax-refuge funds have a natural currency home. LDC and much OECD balance of payments financing has been in one or a combination of international monies: debt issues denominated in the national currency would not be internationally marketable.

The nomadic investor does not become emotionally attached to one money, which then becomes his lifetime standard of value. He is restless: when prospects of stability for one money fade, he searches for alternatives. In the late 1970s, accelerating US inflation caused international investors to decamp increasingly from their dollar bases, and seek shelter and higher real earnings in Deutsche marks, Swiss francs, and gold. Nomads are not regarded favourably by the organizers of ordered societies. Nomadic flows of money were invoked frequently as the source of real economic ills. Some finance ministries suggested the imposition of direct controls: less activist ones considered the nomad problem to be a transient one, due to the supposed lack of alternatives to the dollar as an international money. The nomadic search for new monetary pastures, and its prospects of success, are the subject of the present chapter.

GROWING PAINS

The most popular alternatives to the dollar as an international money have been the Deutsche mark and Swiss franc. From 1977, when the massive Japanese trade surplus emerged, the yen was much sought by international investors. But it is too early to decide whether the yen has the essential property of low real internal risk for it to become a vital component of low risk portfolios, rather than remain a short term speculative instrument.

Growth pains arise from imbalance. Rapid industrialization unaccompanied by social overhead expenditure and rapid internationalization of a money which occurs unevenly among borrowers and lenders give rise to symptoms of the same general condition. As a case study, the Swiss franc is selected here. Two questions are posed: does the small size of the Swiss economy increase the pains of franc growth and does it set a limit to its internationalization?

Swiss franc international

The Swiss franc's attractions as an international investment numeraire have been founded on the reputation of the Swiss National Bank for pursuing zealously price stability, enhanced by a widespread belief in Switzerland's political soundness. Growing international investment demand for the franc caused much greater internal adjustment problems than did the internationalization of the mark. By mid-1978, the real bilaterally trade-weighted appreciation of the Swiss franc over its 1973 base exceeded 30 per cent: that of the Deutsche mark barely reached 5 per cent. The divergence can be explained by the relatively small size of the Swiss economy.

Consider the alternative patterns of exchange rate adjustment generated by investors seeking to switch net $10 billion of the low risk component of their portfolios into Deutsche marks and Swiss francs respectively. The proximate stimulus for the switch could be increased inflation volatility in the US. In the long run, such excess investment demand must be accommodated by an increase in Swiss (or German) debt to foreigners, brought about by continuing basic balance of payments deficit over a long period of time. In the short run, portfolio equilibrium is re-established as a result of the operation of speculation and valuation changes. Speculators short-sell francs to investors when they believe that the franc has risen so far as to generate a satisfactory basic balance of payments deficit flow over subsequent years, and to provide them with a risk return (see *Money, Hard and Soft* pp. 24–7). Lower anticipated returns on francs persuade some investors to delay purchasing Swiss francs even when the ultimately desired weights for currencies in their low risk portfolio have changed in favour of the Swiss franc. An increased risk premium can be gained from continuing to hold dollars of now relatively higher inflation volatility. Similarly some institutions, which report their accounts in dollars, are tempted nevertheless to increase their issue of franc debt by its lower expected effective cost and the fall in inflation volatility measured in francs relative to that in dollars.

As a proportion of GNP, the long-run basic balance of payments adjustment is much larger for Switzerland than for West Germany, and therefore more painful. A greater shrinkage must occur in industries producing traded goods, and a corresponding greater expansion in non-traded goods industries.

A surge in demand for marks causes the dollar exchange rates of other European zone currencies to rise, though by less than that of the mark, so important is West Germany in intra-European trade. Neighbouring countries bear part of the burden of adjustment by switching net exports from non-European zone countries to West Germany; whilst the latter decreases net exports to all countries. Thus all European zone countries contribute significantly towards the correction of the trans-zonal imbalance represented by the desired switch out of dollars into marks.

The emergence of Switzerland as a reserve centre has potentially as much impact as that of West Germany on the dollar exchange rates of neighbouring currencies. A higher proportion of total Swiss trade in goods and services together is with other European countries than is true for West Germany. Therefore a greater proportion of a Swiss than German long-run swing into basic balance of payments deficit (induced by desired inflows from the dollar) will be matched by a swing of net exports of the rest of Europe to the reserve centre. That swing, though, as a percentage of the GNP of the rest of Europe, may not be very different in the Swiss and German illustrations: European GNP outside Switzerland is greater than outside West Germany. The appreciation of the dollar exchange rates of European non-reserve currencies is likely to be similar whether the dollar inflows are into a large or small European reserve centre.

A desired inflow of $10 billion into Swiss francs is about eight times as large a proportion of the Swiss economy as the same size inflow into

Deutsche marks is of the West German economy. However, the impact of a $10 billion inflow into francs on the Swiss franc-dollar rate would be less than eight times the impact of the same size inflow on the mark-dollar rate. The explanation is that each one per cent rise of the Swiss franc against the dollar is considerably more effective in reducing external Swiss payments imbalance than is a one per cent rise of the mark-dollar in reducing German imbalance, where both imbalances are measured as percentages of GNP. Each one per cent rise of the mark against the dollar exerts greater pull than a similar rise of the franc on the dollar exchange rates of neighbouring currencies, so reducing the effective appreciation of the mark more than of the franc.

Where the base economy of a reserve money (francs) is small rather than large the economic impact of a given size inflow of dollars seeking francs as a new low risk home alters as follows:

1. resource shift internally between traded and non-traded goods sectors in the base economy increases,
2. upward shift of dollar exchange rates of other currencies in the same zone as the franc is likely to be of similar order,
3. movement of the dollar exchange rate of the franc is greater.

The greater exchange rate fluctuations to which a small country reserve money is subject detract from its other qualities, and slow its growth rate. Inflows will be halted rapidly by their blowing a fuse: that occurs when the increase in external volatility outweighs the improvement in internal stability which was the origin of the new investment demand for the small reserve money (see p. 59).

Easing franc growth

At various stages in the 1970s, the Swiss National Bank applied brakes to the growth of franc internationalization. Direct controls were placed intermittently on foreign purchases of Swiss franc domestic deposits, bonds, and equities. Long-term maintenance of such controls would be counterproductive. Given the inevitable subjection of the franc to international investment flows, its best protection against high exchange rate volatility is the existence of a large international money and credit market denominated in the Swiss currency.

The wider the international use of the Swiss franc as a component of low risk portfolios and hence of international decision makers' unit of account, the less likely are acute swings in net investment demand that must be speculatively accommodated. Suppose, for example, that a perceived drop in the inflation volatility of Switzerland causes there to be a surge in low-risk ('dreamer') net investment demand for francs. The franc exchange rate rises and franc interest rates fall. Individuals and corporations for whom the franc is an important component of their decision-making unit of account are induced by the falling rates to increase their consumer or physical investment expenditure, so increasing their borrowing demand for francs. The importance of this non-speculative source of supply of franc paper in relieving conditions of investment demand-induced shortage increases with the international numeraire use of the franc. Further, valuation changes caused by any shift of the franc exchange rate should make a greater short-run contribution to satisfying altered portfolio preferences, the larger is the present net investment in francs by non-Swiss. In consequence, the eventual Swiss trade flow accommodation of the inflow can occur over a much longer period of time, and overshooting of interest and exchange rates to tempt speculative absorption is less.

An extreme example demonstrates the significance of size of the international franc market to smooth adjustment to inflows. Suppose 75 per cent of the euro-money and credit markets were denominated in francs. A given desired investment switch of say $10 billion from dollars into francs would affect the franc-dollar exchange rate to a considerably lesser extent than in the present currency make-up of international markets.

Ends hardly ever justify means. Even if the Swiss National Bank accepted the argument that wide international use of its money would provide the best protection against exchange rate volatility, it could still be questioned whether the long period of growth pains on the way was worth the ultimate possible benefit. As the 1980s dawn, there are signs that the National Bank is growing weary of using direct controls to thwart the increasingly inevitable reserve use of the franc.

Minor alternatives to the dollar

The mainstream alternatives to the dollar are well-known; they are the Deutsche mark, Swiss franc, and gold. But what about minor currencies such as the Dutch guilder, or British pound? To date, restrictions on free tradability and non-independence or poor quality of monetary policy have cramped their growth.

Ability to run an independent monetary policy varies between countries. Where the demand for money is found to be a fairly steady function of a few variables whose levels are always readily ascertainable, the running of an independent monetary policy is feasible. The central bank fixes a money supply target, and can thereby control the rate of inflation within target limits. In some countries, though, demand for money functions – and the relation of money supply growth to inflation – is believed to be very unstable. The explanation for such instability is to be found normally either in a non-competitiveness of the local banking structure, or direct quota control of deposit creation. Banking industry and policy structure differences internationally make money supply data more reliable inflationary indicators in some countries than in others.

If a central bank fixed independently a money supply target, and yet the domestic velocity of circulation was unstable and unpredictable, investors would predict that inflation volatility would be high. Central banks of monetary systems blighted with such unstable velocity have a choice between two methods of lowering inflation volatility. First, they may attempt to increase the stability of money demand domestically, by encouraging bank competition and removing quotas and interest rate ceilings. Second, they may decide to pursue an endogenous monetary policy, by pegging the national money to an attractive international money. Domestic inflation volatility could be reduced by so pegging to a money which is favoured with a domestically stable velocity, rather than by announcing an independent target. Such 'imitation monies' are unlikely to gain wide international investment popularity, other than as a poor man's mark, dollar, or franc. The imitation money will normally have to yield a higher interest rate than the genuine, to protect against the risk of the peg being pulled out. The Dutch guilder is an example of an 'imitation mark.' The Canadian dollar is a less obvious example of an 'imitation US dollar.' The Canadian dollar is not pegged to the US dollar, but the polar power of the US money in the North American dollar zone is very strong: Canadian monetary policy is often closely parallel to US policy. Most international investors do not regard the Canadian dollar as a fully independent money.

The velocity of monetary circulation in the UK has been traditionally very unstable. Yet British policy makers in the 1970s did not attempt to reduce inflation volatility by pegging their money to another, such as the mark. The British pound suffered from another disadvantage in international monetary competition – its tradability was restricted. Controls existed that prevented the short-selling of the pound in most contexts. Thus at certain periods, the British pound would be priced inefficiently. Its market price would not then discount the sum of market knowledge, because those with knowledge could be prevented from taking appropriate market action in the form of shorting the pound.

The environment of restricted tradability is not, in general, favourable to the growth of a money as a low risk component of international portfolios. The transactor must be aware that the money is often inefficiently priced, and that there are times at which it is expensive to buy. Every investor must also be a speculator – he cannot count on a body of pure speculators having already swept the paths for him. The international investor who is seeking merely a low risk portfolio is unlikely to assume the task of professional speculation in the British pound. In markets where division of function between speculation and dreamer is not possible, the dreamer is not found normally.

GOLD RENAISSANCE

Since the closing of the US gold window in August 1971, the gold-based monetary system has shrunken to include only its metallic base. In one day, foreign holdings of dollars, which had been previously convertible into gold and so were effectively gold money, became transformed into fiat dollars. The US dollar lost appeal immediately for those investors who had considered it primarily as an interest bearing gold certificate. The fall in the dollar and the sharp rise in the gold price from 1968 onwards was at least partly due to so motivated investment switches.

In the 1970s only one form of gold investment existed – holding the metal itself. With minor exception, credit markets in gold denomination were not to be found. A development to which to look forward in the 1980s is the renaissance of gold credit markets, as outlined in *Money, Hard and Soft* (pp. 148–50). Swiss francs, US dollars, and Deutsche marks, all share one defect as international monies: their base is national, and their values depend on predictions of monetary policies being followed at home. The investor who chooses a paper money as a low risk asset and numeraire must have decided presumably that the issuing central bank's monetary policy is comparatively predictable up to his horizon.

But for long periods ahead national monetary policy is very unpredictable. We do not know today who will be future chairmen of the Swiss, German, and US Central banks, nor to what political pressures they will be subject. The range of rate of increase in already mined gold stocks is bounded more narrowly over long periods of time than the range of rate of increase of paper monies. A review of gold mines and their production potential over, say, the next three decades provides a firmer basis for predicting the rate of growth of mined gold, than a summary of present opinion about central bank politics would provide for predicting paper money growth over the same period.

Gold can be analyzed in terms of its real external and internal risk (see chapter 2, p. 50). Gold is not the national money of any country. Therefore real internal risk cannot be defined in terms of a national price level, but rather as the volatility of the rate of increase in already mined gold supplies. Real external risk of gold has its source in volatility of the real gold exchange rate against the investor's (or borrower's) local money (say francs). A real franc today is a fraction of the nominal franc, equal to the price level in the base year divided by the price level today. A real unit of gold today is defined as a fraction of a nominal unit of gold, equal to the weight of gold above the ground (already mined) in the base year divided by the present comparative weight. The real gold-franc exchange rate is the price of a real franc in terms of a real unit of gold. The real external risk of gold is potentially the highest of all international monies. Changes in the paper money value of gold are an unimportant determinant of paper money demand for world traded commodities.

Over long periods of time, real gold exchange rates are constrained by physical considerations to move within narrower limits than national price levels. Real internal risk becomes a more important consideration than real external risk, and so gold's comparative advantage is its low long-term real internal risk. Gold finds particular favour in the low risk portfolios of investors with long-term horizons.

In effect, international monies can be ranked according to two scales; those of real internal and those of real external risk. On the external scale the ranking in the late 1970s ran from the dollar at the bottom, to the mark, to the Swiss franc, and to gold on top. On the internal scale, for long horizon investors, the ranking in the late 1970s was from gold at the bottom, to the Swiss franc, to the Deutsche mark, to the US dollar.

Euro-gold

The restoration of a credit market in gold should decrease the volatility of the gold price in terms of paper monies. Swings in investor trust of paper monies with national fiat bases would tend to cause flows from euro-marks, dollars, and francs, into gold credit instruments, which shall be termed here euro-gold. Heavy demand for euro-gold would be absorbed in part by its interest yield falling: pressure on the spot gold price would in consequence be less. When investors tended to shift from euro-gold into other euro-monies, its yield would rise: gold borrowers would be discouraged, hence reducing the fall of the metal's price.

Analogously to our Swiss franc analysis, a large euro-gold market would provide the best protection against gold price volatility being induced by investment inflows and outflows. Investors and borrowers who used gold as a unit of account, or a component of their basket unit of account, would increase their issue of gold paper when gold interest rates fell and conversely. Further, the larger are net private holdings of euro-gold, the smaller are likely to be proportionate shifts in net stock demand. Thus a smaller change in the gold price will restore stock equilibrium in the euro-gold market.

Although the development of a gold credit market could decrease the risk of long-term decision-making, who would find it worthwhile to sponsor euro-gold market growth? Any private corporation would consider the initiation of a euro-gold market, by issuing gold de-nominated paper, as a high risk venture. True, there may be social gains from euro-gold initiation, but the corporation would not gain privately thereby. Official institutions would be the probable first initiators of a euro-gold market. Some European governments, for example, hold large gold reserves, which would hedge many times over their probable issue of gold bonds. European institutions such as the European Investment Bank, The European Coal and Steel Community and the EEC itself could be among the first to make gold bond issues. Some LDC governments and other sovereign powers with gold reserves would soon follow the European example.

Speculation in gold

The present gold market consists simply of spot and futures markets in the metal. Long term short-selling of the metal is difficult. A treasurer, who believed that the gold price was artificially high, could not readily issue gold rather than dollar bonds.

Like his paper money counterpart, the gold speculator must make two estimates. First, at the present spot and forward gold prices, how does his projection of the net commercial supply of gold differ from the average market forecast. Net commercial supply is newly mined gold less jewellery and industrial demand. Second, how large is the glacier of net investment overhang for gold? The speculator must calculate whether the prospective net commercial supply of gold will be at a sufficient rate to both melt the glacier overhang and provide a tempting risk premium. The gold speculator here earns his premium by selling gold spot and hoping to buy it back in the future at a premium over present cost that is less than accumulated interest on his interim investment. Larger speculative rewards are earned the greater is the immediate rise in price of gold above its long run marginal cost of physical production (mining). That ratio sets the rate at which investment demand is satisfied with newly mined metal.

The widening of the gold market to include euro-gold would ease the speculative adjustment to changing net investment demand for gold. Speculation need no longer take the ultimate form of present holders of physical metal deciding to sell it spot, in the hope of buying it back profitably. Instead, pure speculators could borrow euro-gold for long maturities.

Not all accommodation to increased net investor demand for gold moves exchange rates. Suppose net demand for all paper money falls equiproportionately, and is matched by the increased net demand for gold. Then a rise in the paper money price of all commodities, and a fall in their gold price, will restore full equilibrium. Need for exchange rate shift arises from non-proportionate shifts out of paper monies or from new demand for gold which is not equiproportional to present holdings across representative portfolios of dollar, mark, and Swiss franc based investors.

Dollars flow into gold

The growth of gold denominated credit markets could be a stabilizing influence on exchange rates between national monies. In chapter 1, it was shown how trans-zonal investment flows between dollars and marks could lead to large changes in trans-zonal exchange rates. Gold, unlike the mark, is not a polar money. Desired shifts of funds from dollars or marks into gold cause much less fluctuation in the mark-dollar and other trans-zonal rates than do desired shifts direct from dollars to marks, or conversely.

Suppose previous dollar holders seek to increase the share of gold in their portfolios. They sell dollars and buy gold. The increase in the investment overhang in the gold market is accommodated by a rise in the gold price (in terms of paper monies) which triggers both some speculative sales of gold by present holders and sales by investors with high gold holdings for whom the re-valued gold proportion in their portfolios is greater than desired. Not all speculative sellers intend to hold dollars during their period of reduced investment in gold. Some particularly those not resident in the dollar zone, will switch to Swiss francs and Deutsche marks. Indeed the temptations are particularly great for the gold speculator to use Swiss francs rather than dollars as their temporary stopping off money, given the suggestion that the franc is often the appropriate speculative numeraire to gold trading (see chapter 2, p. 56). Thus the initial desired switch from dollars to gold by low risk investors triggers eventually some switching from dollars to marks and Swiss francs, but not to the full extent of the gold purchases. Some gold speculators and owners of high gold content portfolios buy dollars.

The impact of a desired switch from dollars to gold in the paper currency markets is thus equivalent to a desired switch from US dollars to a weighted basket of currencies from different zones, including the dollar itself. The trans-zonal impact would be considerably less in volume than the same size flow from dollars to marks.

Gold market intervention

Milton Friedman's suggestion in *The Optimum Quantity of Money*, (Macmillan, 1969) that central bankers desist from 'fine tuning' and instead announce and keep to an immutable money supply growth rate has never won warm reception among policy makers. Paradoxically, central bankers have agreed to an application of the Friedman principle in the gold money market. IMF auctions, and then US Treasury auctions, of gold have effectively acted to increase the supply of privately held growth in an automatic and well-publicised fashion.

The announced intention of US Treasury gold sales was to support the dollar in the foreign exchange markets, rather than to increase the predictability of gold supply and hence the investment attractions of the yellow metal. Gold sales would be absorbed largely by speculators, who anticipated that at the lowered price of gold resulting from gold auctions profit could be made from gradually on-selling to long-term investors. Such speculators would sell currencies to buy gold. Those currencies would be sold for dollars to make payment to the US Treasury. The auctions induced a sale of many currencies, including dollar and mark zone ones, for US dollars. Selling US dollars and dollar zone currencies for dollars is not an effective way of supporting the dollar. The support derived from the auctions was in consequence much less than official sales of European zone and Japanese currencies, on a swap basis, would have been.

Supporting the dollar by gold sales was more powerful than by say, copper sales. Copper is a dollar commodity, and most speculative positions are assumed vis-a-vis dollars, and with dollar financing. Speculative absorption of copper sold at auction would induce preponderantly a sale of dollars for dollars. Gold, in contrast, is a Swiss franc commodity, and speculative positions are financed often in marks and francs. Germany, unlike the US, would find that selling copper stockpiles for marks was more effective than selling gold to support the mark. Speculative absorption of copper would induce a greater sale of dollars for marks than would absorption of gold. Similarly, the UK would not find that tea auctions were a good method of supporting the British pound: tea is a sterling commodity, and inventories would be financed predominately in British currency.

For small countries, the choice of which currency or commodity to sell in support of the domestic money is of less significance. Whether Italy, for example, sells gold, marks, or dollars, to support the lira, the effect on exchange markets is much the same. As the lira is a small currency, intervention in the dollar or mark will affect the lira much more than it will either the dollar or mark. Gold intervention has been demonstrated to be equivalent to mixed mark and dollar currency intervention, and the distinction between the two component types and their mix is unimportant for the lira.

More esoteric than gold

Both gold and Swiss francs are monies for which changes in net investment demand are a relatively large proportion of commercial (or trade) supplies over short to medium periods of time. Econometric models which forecast commercial or trade supplies of metal or currencies respectively are of least aid to the short-term speculator in gold and francs. The popularity of both as components of low risk portfolios depends on the widespread belief that their rate of stock increase will be low.

In the years of recycling OPEC surpluses that followed the quadrupling of the oil price in 1973, the Arab World lacked their own international numeraire. Surpluses were invested predominately in US dollars, and LDCs borrowed dollars to finance their oil-induced deficits. Suppose, instead, that the rulers of Saudi Arabia had decided that they should not put their faith in the American numeraire, and that they would rather coin their own international money over which they would have ultimate control. How could Saudi Arabia have promoted a sufficiently rapid growth in the international use of the riyal? Borrowers would have to have been persuaded to issue riyal-denominated debt instruments. Borrowers and lenders would have needed to be convinced that the volatility of the real value of the riyal in terms of their ultimate purchasing power would be less than of alternative monies over long periods of time.

Riyal based purchasing power is of even less significance than Swiss franc purchasing power in the world commodity markets. Fluctuations in the riyal would not affect world demand for commodities, expressed in other currencies, because riyal-based income is so slight. Oil revenues are not riyal but dollar (or SDR-type) income. Other OPEC members would not have agreed to riyal denomination of the cartel's oil price, because they were concerned with lowering the volatility of oil's purchasing power in the dollar and mark zone economies – with particular emphasis on the zone from where most of their import purchases were made. The real external risk of the riyal would have been potentially greater than that of the Swiss franc given the insignificance of riyal purchasing power in the world. Like with gold, real internal risk of the riyal must be defined as the variability of the rate of increase of the riyal monetary base. An independent riyal price level is hardly identifiable, given the predominance of imported goods in the Saudi consumer market.

The Saudi rulers would have had to out-compete the Swiss in lowering their money's real internal risk, if the riyal was to compete internationally. Suppose they had announced that from now to evermore not one more riyal was to be added or subtracted from the Saudi monetary base. The market would not have believed the Saudi promise, even if all the treasured prayer mats of the Royal Family had been pulled out, and sacred oaths made before Allah. What if revolution was to occur in the desert kingdom? In short, the riyal enjoyed neither the repute of low political risk nor the long record of past inflation performance that would have been essential to its being successfully marketed as a low risk long-term unit of account.

Saudi's rulers would have found it difficult to market the riyal even as an imitation money. Suppose they had considered tying the riyal to the Swiss franc, or Deutsche mark, or US dollar, or gold, or a basket of them all. Product differentiation may have suggested the suitability of a gold peg, and the Saudis would have led the world in a gold renaissance. But Saudi paper would have been of high political risk, and investors would have required a premium return as inducement to bear the risk that a future Saudi Government could break the gold convertibility pledge. Gold-riyal internationalization would have been limited by the re-

luctance of borrowers to pay a risk premium to compensate the lender
against the danger that force majeure of the Saudi Government may
prevent payment in constant gold value. Unless Saudi banks were
particularly low cost in issuing bonds, prime borrowers would have
found it cheaper to issue gold bonds directly, rather than also assuming
the Saudi political risk.

The auction that can't be missed

Some observers may have been surprised by the regular attendance of all
the large bullion houses and Swiss banks at IMF and US Treasury gold
auctions. They can no more afford to miss attending an auction than can
competing supermarkets afford not to partake in a large manufacturer's
special promotion of surplus stock.

Gold sales at auction are eventually absorbed by long-term investment demand. Dealers who bid at auction act as short-term speculators,
intending to on-sell to non-dealer speculators and investors. In
aggregate, dealers (market-makers) find that client purchases exceed
client sales by the amount of gold auctioned. If a large dealer missed an
auction, he would find that his market-making inventory would soon
run down, and he would be forced to restock by buying from dealers
who had attended. Restocking would likely occur at the other dealer's
offer price, and the absentee dealer would suffer a decline in his average
profit per round-trip transaction.

EEC ALTERNATIVES TO THE DOLLAR

The heightened volatility of the US dollar (both internally and
externally) in the late 1970s, provoked an official EEC response.
Momentum developed in plans to limit the fluctuation of intra-EEC
exchange rates. The actual mechanism chosen to achieve that end,
whether the peg is expressed in terms of the mark or the EUA, is less
important than the implications for the pattern of international money
usage.

Any move towards reducing the fluctuation of intra-European
exchange rates would increase the relative attractions of the mark and
Swiss franc compared to the US dollar as Europeans' international
money. The Deutsche mark's real external risk for Frenchmen, Italians,
and Englishmen would be reduced relatively, given the mark's closer
movement with their own money.

The Deutsche mark's use as numeraire in intra-European trade would become more widespread. Closer correlation between dollar exchange rate changes of the mark and French franc, for example, would increase the relative convenience of hedging decisions being made against the mark numeraire (see p. 16). Greater trade use of the mark would broaden both spot and forward exchange markets in marks. Soon prime markets would develop in trading marks against other European currencies rather than just US dollars. It would be cheaper to market-make directly in French francs and British pounds against marks than combining two trades against the dollar numeraire, as at present.

·What are the advantages of schemes to promote lower volatility of intra-European exchange rates and hence the predominance of the mark over the dollar as favorite international money in Europe? First, exchange market transaction costs could be reduced between European currencies, as the mark came to replace the dollar as vehicle currency within Europe. Higher proportions of intra-European trade invoiced in marks would boost turnover in mark exchanges, which together with the reduced volatility of the mark exchange rates of European currencies would reduce the risk of making a market in them against the Deutsche mark rather than against the US dollar. Hence bid-offer spreads should be lower on exchanges of European currencies against marks than against dollars. In 1977–8 during the continuous dollar crises, bid-offer spreads widened considerably on European dollar exchange deals, and on their satellite intra-European exchange transactions. The promotion of the Deutsche mark vehicle should prevent trans-zonal volatility adding to the transaction costs of intra-European zone exchange deals.

A second advantage of limiting by official exchange market intervention intra-European exchange rate fluctuation is to remove the impediment of higher real external risk to the growing usage of the mark, despite its being a lower inflation volatility money than the US dollar. As stated in chapter 2 (p. 50) the dollar has a comparative advantage compared to the mark, due to the larger share of US than West German purchasing power in world trade. That advantage could be eliminated if European currencies became sufficiently coordinated that movements of the mark-dollar rate affected dollar purchasing power in world markets by at least as much as mark purchasing power.

There is a free ride

There is no such thing as a free lunch – so runs the well known motto of the University of Chicago Economics School. But a free lunch is not a free ride, and free rides there are.

Suppose all EEC countries, except, say, Italy, agreed to limit the fluctuation of their currencies against each other. The two mentioned advantages of Deutsche mark promotion – reduction of exchange transaction costs and use of a better unit of account – would still be achieved. Short-term rates of change of the lira-dollar and mark-dollar would become more closely correlated, due to an increase in the proportion of Italian trade with countries whose currencies were pegged to the mark. Thus Italian investors would enjoy the benefits of reduced transaction costs in intra-European trade and the increased attractions of a lower inflation volatility international money, the mark, without the Banca d'Italia committing itself to exchange market intervention.

Condemned to be small

The limiting of European exchange rate fluctuations against the mark could trigger net capital outflows from the smaller cooperating countries. The reduction in the real external volatility of the mark from the viewpoint of most European investors would stimulate a net investment swing into marks from present dollar and local currency holdings. The swing would be particularly large in small countries where international monies have widespread portfolio popularity: balance of payments adjustment problems would ensue. Further, the local money would be considered widely, even by local investors, as an 'imitation mark' and investors would require a risk premium against the possibility that the link with the mark numeraire would be broken. The real cost of local borrowing by domestic enterprises, who must account in the national currency, would be increased.

A school of thought could soon grow that recommended throwing in the nationalist sponge. Why not give up any monetary independence, and reduce the national central bank's status to printing notes and minting coins? These instruments would be exchangeable into marks at par, and would have the same relation to marks as Irish pounds had to British pounds until the late 1970s.

Renouncing national monetary independence, would not remove the special adjustment problems of small European countries situated between large neighbours, such as Benelux (see ch. 1, p. 32). If Benelux governments abdicated monetary sovereignty, in favour of the Deutsche mark, those economies together with West Germany would be subject to money inflow from other European investors. West Germans would welcome Benelux as new entrants to the greater German monetary union, for the brunt of the burden of adjustment to investment flows between marks and dollars would be borne in the Low Countries rather than in Essen, Munster, and Cologne. A higher proportion of Benelux trade and a lower proportion of West German border region trade would now be with non-mark using European countries. Continually shifting trade relations are the price that Benelux would pay for the possible benefit of a smaller long-run net capital outflow.

In practice, in the years since 1973, Benelux central banks have tried to combine some of the advantages of limiting their currencies' fluctuations against the mark whilst permitting sufficient flexibility for their exchange rates to maintain some monetary independence and hence to prevent their economies having to shoulder some of the border adjustment now borne by West German frontier regions. During periods of great mark-dollar volatility, the fluctuations of Benelux currencies against the dollar have been less than those of the Deutsche mark. Yet known ceilings to fluctuations of the Belgian franc and Dutch guilder against the mark have promoted some use of German money in preference to the US dollar by both Benelux borrowers and lenders. Some saving in transaction costs has also been apparent sometimes in Dutch-German exchange markets. During tempestuous times on the dollar-mark axis, prime market-making has occurred in guilders against marks, which has been cheaper than the more normal method of transacting through the vehicle dollar.

Is mark hegemony in Europe inevitable?

Much of the intra-European exchange rate volatility of the 1970s was due to the existence of a basic asymmetry between investment monies. The proportion of international investment interest in relation to the size of the issuing economy was considerably larger for the Swiss franc and Deutsche mark than for the British pound, French franc, and Benelux currencies. If these other countries had followed policies likely to excite international use of their monies, could intra-European exchange rate volatility have been reduced?

Certainly generalized flows out of the dollar due to deteriorating inflation prospects would have been dispersed wider among European monies: their impact on intra-European exchange rates would have been less. But it is also likely that intra-European shifts of capital would have been greater, as the relative attractions of the different European monies varied over time. Whereas the volatility of the mark and Swiss franc against the dollar would have been reduced, that of other European investment monies would probably have increased.

The emergence of a new European alternative to the dollar as an international money would require a coincidence of monetary and political developments. They include a renunciation of national money sovereignty, or deterioration in West Germany's inflationary performance, or decline in West German hegemony in European trade.

Snake crises

In late October 1976, and again in October 1978, a re-alignment occurred of parities within the European Snake. Effectively the Deutsche mark parities of the Dutch guilder and Belgian franc were reduced by two per cent. Yet the question asked by commentators on both occasions was had the mark thereby been revalued? Was the mark likely to open higher against the dollar on the Monday morning, following the decision announced late on Sunday night?

The answer depended on which currency was being sold to support the Benelux monies within the Snake. Suppose the intervention currency had been Deutsche marks. Official mark sales for Belgian francs must depress the mark and raise the franc against the US dollar: the trade-weighted exchange rate of the continental European zone (see p. 22) should be unaffected, as the intervention has no trans-zonal component. When intervention ceases, and the Belgian franc is devalued against the mark, the mark rises against the dollar, but by considerably less than the franc falls. Intervention was much larger proportional to the Belgian than German money markets.

Suppose, instead, that intervention had been in dollars, which had been sold net for Belgian francs. Then the trade-weighted exchange rate of the continental European zone would have risen, as the intervention involved a net trans-zonal flow. When intervention ceases, both the mark and Belgian franc fall against the dollar, but the franc by much more than the dollar. The mark's slight fall against the dollar would be due to Belgium being a significant trade partner of West Germany, and some minor mark adjustment against the dollar is necessary if the German balance of trade is not to be affected by the Belgian move.

CURRENCY ANARCHY

In recent years, the proposal has been made, most notably by Professor Hayek in 'choice in currency' (IEA, 1976), that legal tender laws be abolished. The idea is to increase competition between different monies, and hence provide greater incentive to promotion of stable rates of monetary growth. Those issuers who earned the reputation of maintaining low inflation rates measured in their currency, would obtain the largest monetary constituencies. The Hayek proposal can be criticized for both ignoring transaction costs in monetary exchange markets and failing to distinguish inflation from exchange risk. The crucial influence of such costs on monetary choice is now demonstrated with two case studies, Andorra and Benelux.

Andorra: competition in practice

Andorra is a principality lying high in the Pyrennees between France and Spain. The main town, Andorra-la-Veille, is much more easily approachable from Spain than from France. The President of France and the Bishop of Seo de Urgel (Spain), as co-princes, are charged with the conduct of foreign affairs, defence, and the judicial system. A ruling General Council is in charge of local administration. No duty or tax is charged on consumer sales, and so Andorra has developed into an active duty free shopping centre. No exchange controls exist in Andorra. Andorra's claim to fame is that two monies are legal tender, the French franc and Spanish peseta. A shopper can request change in either legal tender presented, and can ask for price quotations in both. When arriving at a hotel, the receptionist will ask whether payment is to be made in pesetas or francs, and quote accordingly.

Check-in accounts may be opened with banks in both francs and pesetas, which may be debited and credited with French and Spanish banknotes respectively at par. Dual currency current account banking is possible in Andorra, because both are employed for transactions purposes: and commercial banks operating there can dispose of banknotes readily in exchange for bank deposits of the same denomination.

Yet, despite the French franc being a lower inflation volatility money than the Spanish peseta, the latter has become the predominant medium of exchange in Andorra. Supermarkets price their merchandise in pesetas, and their cash registers operate in pesetas. The shopper who uses franc banknotes will be quoted a franc price which is calculated on the basis of the going banknote dealer offer rate of pesetas per franc, and thus he pays for the assumed transaction costs that the shop would incur in selling the francs for pesetas. Wages are denominated in pesetas, as are public utility charges.

The reason for the peseta's predominance as Andorra's medium of exchange is to be found in a combination of transaction cost and exchange risk considerations. Because Andorra-la-Veille is more accessible from the Spanish than the French side of the mountain range, goods tend to be bought from Spanish suppliers, and a large proportion of shoppers come from Spain. An Andorra shop is more likely to find an excess of franc than peseta receipts relative to its payment requirements: further, the low volume of payments and receipts in francs means a less economical use of its franc than peseta current account. Hence the transaction cost of exchange is weighted on the French franc rather than the peseta price of goods.

Merchandise sold in Andorra can mostly be described as 'peseta goods' (see figure 2.2). They are purchased in Spain, and in the short-run their peseta price is much less sensitive than their French franc price to changes in the peseta-French franc exchange rate. From the viewpoint of Andorra residents, the real external risk of the peseta is less than that of the franc. So the peseta is the chosen unit of account for most short term contracts, including wages and consumer prices, despite its higher real internal risk compared to the French franc.

As a longer term store of value, the functions of the Spanish peseta and the French franc in Andorra are reversed, with French franc savings accounts being more popular than peseta accounts. Real internal risk is of greater importance in long maturity monetary choice. For medium maturities the French franc is advantageous compared to still lower real internal risk currencies, because their real external risk is higher: the Andorran's spending is concentrated more heavily on French franc than Deutsche mark goods.

Benelux experiment

Although the Andorra case study may be regarded as esoteric, certain insights are gained as to how monetary competition would operate in small continental countries. The study suggests that the dominant medium of exchange would prove to be that of the largest trading partner. Hayekian competition, based on differing inflation performances, would determine patterns of currency usage only for long-term contracts and savings.

Suppose Benelux countries had no legal tender laws and did not print their own money. Assume further an initial monetary vacuum, which competitors must fill. Competition would take the form of each region, or county, deciding which of alternative monies to use as its medium of exchange.

Towns near the German border would not hesitate in choosing marks, as the highest proportion of their trade would be with Germany rather than with other regions of Belgium or with France. Similarly, areas near the French border would use the French franc.

German trade is much greater than French trade with Benelux (see table 1.2) and the mark would make greater inroads beyond the immediate border regions than the French franc. Hence the hinterland of Benelux would quickly become mark dominated. Once mark predominance was established in the border regions of Groningen, Gelderland, Limburg, and Liege, the impetus for a further mark thrust would be established. For then inner regions, such as Friesland, Utrecht, Antwerpen, and Brabant would now be trading predominately with mark-using partners, whether in Germany itself, or the mark border regions of Benelux. Meanwhile further penetration of the French franc would stop dead beyond the border regions of Hainault and Namur. Inner regions would find the proportion of their trade with Germany or mark-Benelux regions increasing much more rapidly than with France or franc-Benelux regions, so they would be swayed in turn to choose the mark. Benelux monetary independence is the dyke built against inundation by the Deutsche mark sea.

Genuine monetary competition would follow from the abolition of legal tender laws in large countries only or in islands. Elsewhere, resignation of national monetary promotion would create the hole in the dyke that would allow the country to be flooded by the nearest large money. Islands do not have border regions, through which the dominant money could filter into the hinterland. Large countries have a lower proportion of external trade than small ones, and border region penetration would be both less likely and less significant in determining hinterland monetary choice.

POLITICAL RISK

So far, international currency choice has been discussed in terms of real external and real internal risk. Political risk should also be considered. Political risk measures the probability of a borrower being forced to default because of the imposition of exchange or other controls by a political authority.

Three dimensions of risk

Political risk in international money and capital markets is 3-dimensional. Consider the three types of risk relevant to a borrower resident in Italy. First, Italy may place restrictions on payments to non-residents. Second, restrictions could be placed on payments to residents, in the event of political revolution in Italy. Third, the currency used to denominate the international borrowing may be subject to independent political risk. For example if the borrowing was in US dollars, the lender would have to consider the risk that US regulations may in the future inhibit the payment of dollars to foreigners, or create a special financial rate of exchange for the dollar.

Dimensions of political risk are illustrated in figure 3.1. Of the examples given, only the risk of the euro-dollar deposit in Rome is three-dimensional. The Swiss cantonal bond and US Treasury bond's political risk are one-dimensional: the only risk to be considered is the imposition of controls in the borrower's country, whose currency is also used as denominator. Euro-currency loans are denominated in a different currency from that of the granting bank's residence, and hence their political risk is usually at least two-dimensional.

One-dimensional Swiss risk

The dimensional framework illustrates why domestic entities can often borrow more cheaply in the local than foreign money. If a Swiss canton for example, was to raise dollar finance it may have to pay a premium against the risk of inconvertibility of non-resident dollars, such as occurred during World War Two. Such a premium is not payable on Swiss franc borrowing, because the risk of inconvertibility is assumed to be zero.

The Swiss franc's zero risk of inconvertibility adds to its attraction as a unit of account in international credit markets. Suppose the Austrian Government is considering whether to raise finance in US dollars, Deutsche marks, or Swiss francs – the three international monies. Only by choosing Swiss francs can the Austrian Government avoid adding a second dimension of political risk to its borrowing. In dollars or marks, the lender would require a premium to cover both the risk of Austria restricting payments to non-residents, and of the US or West Germany acting similarly.

In general, a currency's risk of inconvertibility, or being divided into two tiers, must be very low if it is to become popular as an international

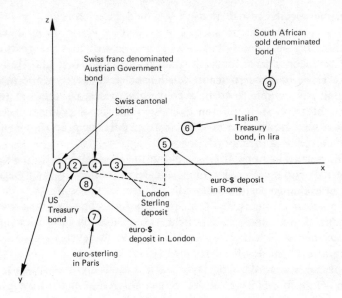

Figure 3.1 Dimensions of Political Risk

Notes: (1) x – axis measures the risk that payments to non-residents may be restricted
by country of borrower
y – axis measures the risk that payments may be restricted to non-
residents, or a 2-tier exchange market established, by country of issue of
the money used to denominate the borrowing
z – axis measures the risk that payments may be restricted to both residents
and non-residents by country of the borrower
(2) 1, 2, 3, 4 are on the x – axis
6, 9 on the xz plane
7, 8 on the xy plane
5 has non-zero x, y, z coefficients

unit of account. Even if the Banca d'Italia's inflation record came to
equal that of the Swiss National Bank, the franc would have a
comparative advantage to the lira as an international money.

Safest at home?

Home is not safest for all. The risk of domestic political revolution and
confiscation is considerable in many parts of the world. Investors from
such countries cannot exclude political risk from their monetary
portfolios, however hard they try. More precisely, they cannot by

investing locally ensure that they would be unaffected by inconvertibility or other disturbances. For example, a Mexican who invested
in domestic peso bonds must recognize the risk that the peso may
become inconvertible for both residents and non-residents. He may,
however, be less concerned about such risk than the foreigner because at
least he will be able to spend inconvertible pesos on domestic goods
inside Mexico. Such differences in significance of political risk for
residents and non-residents help to explain differing proportions of the
local currency in their portfolios.

The particular popularity of gold in the international portfolios of
residents of politically risky countries can be explained by their inability
to invest in a domestic money which is free of political risk from the
viewpoint of residents. Gold bullion in a Swiss bank vault, or Swiss
cantonal bearer bonds, must be held in compensation if overall political
risk of their wealth holdings is to be reduced to levels that would be
acceptable to those in less troubled lands.

The importance of political risk considerations in currency choice has
been demonstrated in recent banking crises. At the time of the Credit
Suisse Chiasso crisis in Spring 1977, the franc slumped as investors
became anxious about the safety of Swiss banks. In autumn 1975, at the
height of the New York City bankruptcy threat, flight from the US
dollar depressed it in the foreign exchange markets. International
investors were fearful that if New York City defaulted on its debts,
several large US banks would face liquidity problems. The risk of US
domestic dollar deposits was perceived to have increased.

Similarly, if massive LDC debt defaults were to occur, US banks
would be most adversely affected, since they have been the heaviest
lenders there. The perceived risk of US dollar deposits with domestic
US banks and their foreign branches would increase. Investors who are
concerned to maintain a low level of default (political) risk, and
therefore shun euro-currency deposits on which such risk is usually two-
dimensional, would switch to holding domestic deposits in Switzerland
and Germany, and to holding gold. Downward pressure on the US
dollar would result, and the Swiss franc, Deutsche mark, and gold price
would rise.

Gold and political crisis

The anatomy of world wide political crisis would differ today from that
at the beginning of the twentieth century. In the repeated war scares up
to 1914, the typical response of world financial markets included an

upward move of interest rates on all major monies. The perceived increased political risk of paper national monies would lead investors to switch into metallic gold. But national monies were pegged to gold and hence changed preferences were accommodated by interest rates rising on such paper gold deposits. Thus political crisis could mean a sharp deflationary impact.

Today, when gold floats against other monies, a world political crisis would have a different financial impact. The Swiss franc, gold, and some other storable commodities would jump in price. National money interest rates would be much less affected.

Gold, like Swiss francs, is of zero political risk, which adds to its attractions as a potential international numeraire. The political risk of gold bonds, like that of Swiss franc bonds, is zero in the dimension of currency inconvertibility. It follows that gold is the only denomination other than francs in which a Swiss entity could borrow internationally without paying a premium for additional political risk. Similarly, non-Swiss borrowers should find gold and francs are the only international monies (other than their own) in which they can borrow without adding a further premium cost to cover another dimension of political risk.

Halo effects

A feature of international currency choice has been the prominence of less-than-top credit risk borrowers in the new issue bond markets of currencies subject to particularly heavy investment demand. In early 1978, when new net investor demand for Deutsche marks was running at very high levels, the share of LDC borrowing in that sector leaped ahead. Heavy demand for Deutsche marks had led to sharply lower Deutsche mark bond yields and interest rates. It is a familiar property of investor behaviour, which can be rationalized by assuming the existence of risk aversion and that risk is entirely measurable by variance of the probability distribution of returns, that a general lowering of yields will cause investors to increase the proportion of risky securities in their portfolio. When risk premiums within the mark sector decrease, as occurs when mark denominated asset yields fall, high risk borrowers account for a larger share of new issue mark markets.

Generally, corporate and state treasurers should pay close attention to changing fashions in international currency taste. Suppose the Deutsche mark is gaining in popularity relative to the US dollar. The number of investors holding portfolios entirely consisting of non-dollar currencies will then be increasing. If a corporation or government did not correspondingly increase its Deutsche mark borrowing and decrease its US dollar borrowing it would find that it was selling its name risk to a shrinking number of portfolios: it would have to pay an increasing risk premium cost. Its name would become relatively scarce in the growing number of wholly non-dollar portfolios, and the corporation or government would find that it could borrow in such currencies at a lower real rate. Heterogeneity of investor currency taste should so encourage corporations and governments to spread their borrowing between different currencies.

Political and default risk considerations have been shown to have important implications for currency choice by both borrower and lender. In chapter 6 it shall be shown how political risk affects competition in the euro-banking system.

4 Two Tiers – and a Black Market

In Ancient Rome, there was a temple to Janus supposed to have been built by Numa which was always open in times of war and shut in times of peace. Livy recorded that in the period of seven hundred years from its construction to the reign of Augustus, the temple was closed for only two short intervals – after the first Punic War, and after Octavian's victory at Actium in 31BC.

In the time that has elapsed since the breakdown of the international gold standard in 1914, the stretches of time during which all major currencies have been free of restrictions on tradability, whether aimed at inflows or outflows, have been short. Black markets, two-tier credit markets, are the norm of the world of paper monies, just as War was the normal state of Ancient Rome. The international investor should be familiar with the properties of black and two-tiered markets, and not consider them as exceptions from a unified norm.

TRADING BANKNOTES

Governmental controls on the international flow of money are least effective against the transfer of bearer instruments. The most commonly found bearer instrument is the banknote. Many types of relationship are possible between foreign banknote markets and the domestic foreign exchange market, and they are the subject of the present section.

Inconvertible banknotes

In banknote market analysis, it is useful to distinguish convertible from non-convertible notes. Banknotes are convertible if they may be re-imported without restriction into the country of origin and credited to convertible bank deposits there. In the 1970s, the major non-convertible notes in Western Europe were Spanish pesetas and Italian lira. British pound, Dutch guilder, Swiss franc, French franc and Deutsche mark banknotes were all convertible.

The Italian lira is taken here as an example of a currency whose banknotes are inconvertible. There are two main sources of lira banknotes to markets outside Italy. First, lira banknotes are bought from Italian banks in exchange for convertible non-lira currency deposits. Second, Italians smuggle lira notes to foreign centres, as one method of exporting capital. There are two main categories of lira purchasers outside of Italy. First, tourists purchase amounts up to a legal limit to bring into Italy and spend them on their vacations. Second, smugglers exceed the legal limits and spend the notes on buying goods, including vacations. The diplomatic bag is one vehicle for such operations.

During winter months, when illicit capital exports tend to exceed tourist demand for lira notes, the banknote rate for liras can fall sometimes to heavy discounts below the official lira rate. Further, Italian political crises in recent years have occurred outside the tourist season, aggravating the excess supply of lira banknotes in external markets during the winter and spring. In early 1978, the discount of the banknote quote in Lugano was sometimes more than 10 per cent below the official Milan quote.

Heavy outflows of banknotes are absorbed in two ways. First, a widening discount increases the rewards to re-entry smuggling, so that such operations increase in scope. Second, speculators buy lira notes in the expectation that the discount will narrow as natural tourist demand and smugglers absorb gradually the external lira float. This kind of speculation is inhibited by the high cost of borrowing euro-liras to finance lira banknote inventories: the cost of euro-lira finance has often exceeded 20 per cent per annum. The higher are euro-lira rates, the greater will be the impact of lira note outflows on the banknote discount and the quicker will be the rate of re-smuggling them into Italy, so reducing sharply demand for liras in the official foreign exchange market.

There are two black markets in liras, one outside Italy and one inside. Inside Italy, foreigners can sell convertible banknotes for liras in unofficial markets at rates of exchange often superior to the official. The relation of the black market price in Italy to that in Switzerland depends on a balance of risk considerations. If the policing of note exports were particularly effective, then many Italians may accept a lower price in Italy for lira notes than that quoted in Lugano: large denomination foreign notes are easier to conceal on exit from Italy than are stacks of liras. If the policing of lira note imports into Italy were also tight, then the Lugano market may dry up entirely, unable to compete with the domestic black market. Lastly, black market trading inside Italy is itself risky. Customs officials attempt to screen whether convertible banknotes brought in by foreigners were exchanged in the official market. In principle, any shortfall of convertible banknotes on exit below the level on entry must be reconciled for each passenger by evidence of official exchange transactions. If this last police activity was the most effective of all, then it is unlikely that the domestic lira black market could compete with the Lugano market.

During the summer months, the net demand for lira notes in external markets by foreign tourists outweighs commonly the supply of notes by Italian exporters of capital. The banknote rate then tends to rise above the official rate, and banks in foreign centres replenish their inventories of lira banknotes by buying supplies either directly or indirectly from Italian banks. Purchases are made at the official lira-dollar rate, and transport costs are paid by the buyer. Most foreign banks experience some difficulty in engaging in such direct transactions with Italy, and prefer to deal where possible with Swiss banks whose delivery dates are more reliable.

Peseta siphon

The structure of the peseta banknote market differs in one key respect from that of the lira market. Although peseta notes are inconvertible, Andorra provides a mechanism for siphoning legally peseta banknotes back into Spain. Andorra banks may ship peseta notes to Spain and credit them there to special 'Andorra peseta' accounts with correspondent banks. These accounts may be used to purchase goods in Spain for export to Andorra.

In theory, three exchange rates should be identifiable – for the Andorra peseta, the official peseta, and the black market (banknote) peseta. Goods and money arbitrage via Andorra restricts in practice the differentials between the three rates. If the Andorra peseta fell to a steep discount below the official Spanish peseta, some foreign importers from Spain would switch to buying Andorra rather than official pesetas and have goods shipped through Andorra to their ultimate destination. If the banknote peseta rate fell below the Andorra rate, then Andorra banks could arbitrage profitably by buying pesetas in the external black market and shipping them to Spain where they would be transformed into Andorra pesetas.

Banknote markets: wholesale and retail

In Greek mythology, centaurs were half human and half horse. Analogously banknote market structure shares some of the features of both commodity and currency deposit exchange markets. The similarity with commodity market structure is due to the significance of transport and storage costs in banknote markets. The link with currency deposit exchanges is attributable to the possibility of transforming banknotes into bank deposits.

Dealing spreads are typically wider in banknote than currency deposit exchange markets. Banknotes yield no interest, and storage and insurance costs can be substantial. Banknote dealers quote therefore higher spreads than their bank deposit counterparts. Both a retail and wholesale banknote market may be identified. On large deals in convertible banknotes, quoted spreads are reduced: the office costs of executing a transaction do not increase proportionately with the size of transaction. On large deals in inconvertible banknotes, quoted spreads may increase despite the proportional reduction in attributable office costs: the inconvertible note dealer does not have the option of shipping notes back to the country of origin and hence he is concerned about the risk of substantial inventory building up.

The banknote retailer must hold inventory on his premises and perform some market-making function. Unlike in the currency deposit exchange market, all retail orders (at whichever branch office received) cannot be passed through the one head office market-maker, and satisfied from the inventory centralized there. Banknote retailers use their wholesaler, which is often the main office of their banking group in the region, as the marginal source and disposal unit for replenishing or disposing of inventory. It would be unprofitable for the retailer to satisfy each transaction by dispatching a van to the wholesaler. The economics of transport costs, amongst which must be included speed of delivery, suggests that the retailer should set a minimum value to the volume of banknotes which he will transact with the wholesaler. The retailer will also set a maximum value, depending on market conditions, to the volume of inventory which he aims to hold. The retailer does not enjoy the high volume business of the wholesaler, and he could not quote competitively a dealing spread that would justify the risk of large inventory holding.

Should a particular banknote retailer in Amsterdam, Mr. B, find that his inventory of Deutsche mark banknotes is building up excessively, he would find it more profitable to dispose of those inventories to his wholesaler than to reduce his own bid and offer rates to levels well below those quoted by competing retailers. The wholesaler has a wider network of high volume clients and hence faces a more elastic demand for notes than the retailer.

Entrepot wholesale trade in convertible banknotes

The wholesaler's bid and offer quotes in any centre must lie within a range whose boundaries are determined by the costs of transporting notes to or from the country of issue. Suppose the interbank currency deposit exchange rate between Deutsche marks and Dutch guilders, quoted both in Amsterdam and Frankfurt, is 1.0835–65 Dfl/Dm. Suppose further, that the transport costs of shipping notes from Amsterdam to the nearest German frontier town, Wesel, is 0.0030 % for typical wholesale volumes. Then a boundary quote for Amsterdam banknote rates, within which actual quotes must lie, is 1.0805–95 Dfl/Dm. A normal dealing spread on wholesale note transactions is 0.0050 per cent. Thus an observed Amsterdam wholesale quote of 1.0845–95 Dfl/Dm would indicate that trading was having a one-way bias, with more buyers than sellers of mark notes, the balance being met by supplies bought from German banks.

The banknote rate in one centre is constrained also within a range determined by banknote quotes in other centres. For example, the wholesale offer price of British pound banknotes (in terms of dollar bank deposits) in Amsterdam must not be greater than the offer price of British pound notes in Brussels plus the cost of note shipment from Brussels to Amsterdam. Thus a whole series of boundary quotes can be identified for Amsterdam Deutsche mark banknote trading, including a Brussels, London, Paris, and German frontier one. The *effective boundary quotes* in Amsterdam are the keenest bid and offer rates which can be selected from all boundary quotes.

Important wholesale banknote centres may be identified in major commercial cities throughout Western Europe. At any point in time, an effective boundary quote can be identified for each denomination of banknote market in each centre. Wholesale markets which occupy a geographically central position, and within low cost reach of many other markets, will tend to provide most often an effective boundary quote in these centres. Amsterdam occupies a prominent position in the structure of Northern Europe's banknote markets. It is central with respect to busy centres in Belgium, France, West Germany, down the Rhine to Switzerland, and northwards to the United Kingdom and

Scandinavia. Therefore the Amsterdam boundary quote is often an effective one in Northern European banknote market places. It should also be expected that the market which is most often an effective boundary is also most often the external source or disposal point of banknotes. When, for example, the wholesale offer rate of British pounds in Paris rises to the effective boundary ceiling set by Amsterdam, Paris wholesalers will switch their marginal source of supply to there.

Amsterdam's natural tendency to being the marginal source or absorber of banknotes for Northern European markets has been the basis for its development of entrepot trade. The Dutch skill in developing entrepot business, particularly in oil and postal services, has been extended to banknotes. Amsterdam has two principal advantages compared to London as Northern Europe's banknote entrepot centre. First, its geographic position is more central. Second, Amsterdam, unlike London, is not separated from other countries by the sea. Sea transport is slow. Air transport involves delays at entry and exit, and often necessitates third party handling with associated high costs of insurance. In contrast, shipments of notes can leave and arrive in Amsterdam in the unrelinquished charge of the note dealer's own security personnel, and in his own transport vehicles.

Security risks explain the inability of certain West German centres to develop entrepot trade in banknotes. Risks of theft in Germany are considered high, and insurance costs of inventory are consequently high. The wider bid-offer spreads that result in West German wholesale markets place them at a comparative disadvantage with Amsterdam.

The entrepot trader acts as both speculator and arbitrager. As arbitrager, he buys British pounds in Paris, for example, and ships them to Brussels, when the offer rate in the Belgian capital has risen above the Paris boundary quote. Action is motivated by presently available profit opportunities. As speculator, the Amsterdam entrepot trader, Mr. Exim, buys British pounds in Zurich when their Swiss price is depressed relative to their price elsewhere, although pure arbitrage is not possible. Mr. Exim believes that within a short period, British pounds will become relatively expensive in one of the northern European centres within easy reach of Amsterdam. Mr. Exim intends to hold his Swiss purchases in inventory ready to profit from a neighbouring shortage. By assuming such risk positions, Mr. Exim is arbitraging essentially between probability distributions. He buys in Switzerland today in the expectation that soon an actual arbitrage opportunity will occur, say in Bremen, whereby the difference between the sale price and purchase price is more than the sum of transport costs from Zurich to Amsterdam to Bremen.

Mr. Exim, like other entrepot traders in Amsterdam, develops business contacts with wholesale banknote market-makers in other centres, who will frequently request him to quote for orders. Mr. Exim builds up his clientele by gaining a reputation for being able often to out-compete offers from other centres. Geographic position and enterprise of its traders are the source of Amsterdam's success.

In the example of Mr. Exim buying British pounds in Switzerland, the Amsterdam wholesale offer price of pounds must equal the Zurich offer price plus transport costs to Amsterdam. If the Amsterdam wholesale price were initially less than the Zurich boundary price, Mr. Exim would have embarked on the speculative entrepot operation mentioned above by buying up pound notes in Amsterdam, until their price had reached the boundary ceiling. Thus banknote prices in an entrepot centre are more subject to international influences than in a centre specialising in local trade.

Market heart in Switzerland

Switzerland is at the heart of the international banknote market. That country's twin features of high volume two-way tourist trade plus popular international investor banking services enable Swiss banknote market-makers to operate on dealing spreads that are narrower generally than in other centres. Even so, Switzerland tends to suffer from one way tendencies. There are often more natural sellers than natural buyers of foreign banknotes. Swiss dealers must often dispose of surplus foreign notes in other centres. Foreign note prices in Switzerland are then relatively low and neighbouring centres in Italy, France, and Germany, will find it cheaper to buy banknotes in Switzerland and ship them than to buy them in the country of origin and pay the transport costs from there. Amsterdam entrepot traders play a key role in the disposal of Swiss surpluses of foreign banknotes throughout their northern European network.

As Switzerland is so frequently the marginal supplier of banknotes to other centres, a close network of business contacts has developed between wholesale dealers inside and outside of that country. It is routine for non-Swiss dealers to seek quotes in Switzerland. Despite a one-way trading bias, the size and depth of the Swiss market so ensure that it remains the heart of the international market, of which many other banknote centres are associates. Swiss dealers can remain confident that they will not have to offload their frequent surplus of foreign banknotes at the buyers' bid rate in other markets. Rather, continual wholesale demand from other smaller centres offsets Switzerland's natural bias.

Banknotes cheap and dear

Certain denominations of banknotes tend to be cheap relative to bank deposits. For example, during summer months, tourist demand for Deutsche mark banknotes falls far short of Deutsche mark note sales by German tourists abroad in exchange for local banknotes. The wholesale banknote bid rate in foreign centres then tends to equate the interbank currency deposit bid rate for marks minus the cost of shipping notes back to Germany. Suppose that the interbank deposit exchange rate for marks against French francs is 2.1750–2.1780 Ff/Dm, and the wholesale cost of shipping notes from Nice to Germany is 0.0035 per cent. The summer glut of mark notes in the South of France would suggest that the wholesale banknote quote there would be 2.1715–2.1765 Ff/Dm. During the winter months, mark banknotes can be transitorily in short supply. Then, for the same interbank deposit quote, the wholesale banknote rate could rise to 2.1765–2.1815 Ff/Dm, or $\frac{1}{4}$ per cent above the summer rate. Costs of storage inhibit speculators from evening out such seasonal swings in the banknote markets.

In conditions of pervasive one-way trade, mark wholesale banknote rates inside Germany would tend to equal those outside. In the summer, the French franc wholesale banknote offer quote in, say, Frankfurt, would equal the interbank offer rate for French francs plus the cost of shipment from France, making 2.1715 Ff/Dm. The two-way wholesale quote in Frankfurt would be 2.1715–65 Ff/Dm, close to quotes in France. The banknote transactor should expect to gain little from buying francs against marks in France rather than in Germany, when trade has a one-way direction. When, however, trade is about equal in both directions, the banknote rate is likely to vary significantly between centres. For example, a glut of French francs in Frankfurt may transitorily co-exist with a glut of Deutsche marks in Paris. Then the Paris and Frankfurt quotes could consistently be 2.1715–65 Ff/Dm and 2.1765–2.1815 Ff/Dm respectively. An incentive is so created for German visitors to France to change their money in Frankfurt before departure, and similarly for the French visitor to Germany. The costs of cross-hauling banknotes between centres are so avoided.

Zurich 1923

The German hyperinflationary experience after World War One provides a test for many propositions in monetary economics, including those about the structure of banknote markets. Throughout the hyperinflation the German authorities restricted banks in Germany from selling foreign banknotes, so operating a type of exchange control. In practice, the regulations were of limited effectiveness, and unofficial markets in foreign notes grew up throughout the country. In addition, black markets outside Germany, notably in Switzerland, developed where mark banknotes could be sold for foreign banknotes.

As inflation worsened, the transaction costs of dealing in the black markets, particularly those situated outside Germany, became enormous. Bresciani-Turroni in *Economics of Inflation* (Kelley, 1968), recounts that on November 5, 1923, mark banknotes were quoted in Zurich at 0.50–3.50 francs/1 billion marks. Dealing spreads were wide because of the great volatility of the mark exchange rate. Spreads were wider in Zurich than in Berlin, because the mark note dealer in Zurich had to hold an inventory of marks on which no interest would be earned – while daily mark interest rates were over 100 per cent per annum in the latter stages of the hyperinflation. The black market dealer inside Germany, in contrast, would finance an inventory of foreign banknotes by borrowing marks and so he escaped the levying of inflation tax.

The rates quoted for paper marks would generally be lower in Zurich than in Berlin. The outpouring of mark banknotes into Switzerland exceeded natural tourist and travel demand. A balance of banknotes had to be shipped back to Germany by professional operators. But the erosion of value of the banknotes during the period of shipment to Germany could be substantial. Hence dealers in Zurich would pay a Swiss franc price for mark notes today influenced by their estimate of what the telegraphic mark rate would be at the time of their entry into Germany. Similarly, buyers of mark notes in Zurich would not pay a price higher than their estimate of the exchange rate at their time of spending in Germany. Yet some Germans preferred to sell marks in Zurich, rather than at the higher rates inside Germany, because of the risks associated with black market dealings there.

Banknotes large and small

Banknotes are not homogeneous: they come in different shapes and sizes. Supply and demand conditions can vary for, say, large and medium size Swiss franc notes in London, and their quoted pound rates can differ. Elasticity of substitution between sizes is in reality small, and price differences limited. In general, large denomination notes command higher prices than small where shipment back to country of origin occurs frequently: per unit value transport costs decline with size of denomination. Thus large denomination French franc notes sell for premiums over small ones in Geneva and Bale. Where shipment from country of origin occurs frequently, the reverse relation holds. In London, supplies of Swiss franc banknotes must often be replenished from Switzerland. Hence large denomination Swiss franc notes are usually cheaper to buy than small ones in London, their cost of shipment being less.

Setting the maximum denomination banknote is a policy issue to be resolved by each central bank. Those which restrict the international tradability of their money are normally reluctant to issue large denominations, fearing to facilitate thereby the smuggling of money across their frontiers. Hard money central banks, in contrast, hope to gain seigniorage from widespread hoarding of their notes. A low inflation money available in large denomination form is also an attractive means of payment in the grey areas of the world marketplace.

TWO-TIER MONEY

There are two basic market structures that can be erected by central banks and governments for controlling the international flow of money across their frontiers. They are the two-tier credit market and the two-tier exchange market. In a two-tier credit market, residents deal freely with each other in one tier, and non-residents deal freely with each other in the second tier. Credit transactions between resident and non-resident are controlled. In a two-tier exchange market, commercial transactions (arising out of payment for goods and services) are effected in one tier, whilst financial transactions (arising out of payment for securities and direct investments) are effected in the second tier.

Two-tier credit market

A two-tier credit market is typified by the coexistence of an uncontrolled euro-market and a domestic market to which access is controlled according to the residence of the transactor. Arbitrage is limited between the two tiers and substantial interest rate differentials are possible between the two.

The Swiss franc credit market has been two-tiered for most of the 1970s. Severe restrictions prevented non-residents from lending in the domestic Swiss credit market, directly or indirectly. Non-residents would be able to lend indirectly to Swiss residents if the latter could borrow in the euro-Swiss franc market, where funds are lent commonly by non-residents. National Bank regulations have inhibited in principle such activity.

The British pound credit market has been tiered, but in the opposite direction to the Swiss example. Non-resident borrowing is curtailed in the domestic pound market, and restrictions on UK resident lending in the euro-pound markets prevent non-residents from borrowing indirectly domestic pounds.

The influence of two-tier credit markets on the exchange rate depends on the driving of a wedge between domestic and euro-interest rates. For example, suppose that a sudden deterioration in US inflation prospects causes a surge in investor demand for Swiss francs. The two-tier structure of the franc credit market should ensure that investor demand is deflected wholly to the euro sector, where interest rates should fall to substantially lower levels than if some absorption could occur in the domestic sector. This low level of interest rates discourages would-be investors in francs, and upward pressure on the exchange rate is eased.

Tiering a credit market is less exchange rate effective when interest rates in the domestic market are already at a very low level. For example, the Swiss National Bank increased in early 1978 the barriers between the euro and domestic Swiss franc credit markets. The controls were imposed when money market rates in Switzerland were at a record low of $1-1\frac{1}{2}$ per cent. That allowed only a theoretical 1 per cent maximum for the euro-domestic Swiss franc interest rate differential. In practice, the differential could not exceed $\frac{1}{2}$ per cent: most investors would rather hold Swiss banknotes in a safebox than deposit them with a eurobank to earn less than $\frac{1}{2}$ per cent.

Tiering of the Swiss franc credit market should not be considered a permanent feature of the international monetary landscape. Net investment demand for euro-Swiss francs is at present being satisfied in part by corporations and governments on the basis of speculative judgement. They believe that the Swiss franc has risen so high that in the longer term Switzerland will run a basic balance of payments deficit. When that happens they will start closing their franc debt exposure at a profit.

The displacing of short-run speculative accommodation by adjustment through the Swiss basic balance – essential to the longer term stability of the franc exchange market – would be hindered if the present tiered structure of the franc credit market was maintained. The present tiering would prevent Swiss residents borrowing francs from non-residents. Therefore they could not replace speculators as issuers of franc debt to long run investors when the Swiss basic balance swung into deficit.

Two-tier exchange market

Two-tier currency markets are characterized by division according to the purpose of the transaction, rather than by residence of the transactor. The Belgian franc exchange market is a good example of a tiered structure. Commercial payments for goods and services must be executed in the 'convertible' tier of the franc currency market: foreigners must pay for Belgian exports with convertible francs, and Belgians buy foreign currency for imports in the convertible tier. Exchange transactions with their origin in investment sales or purchases must be effected in the financier tier by both Belgians and non-Belgians.

A major aim of instituting a two-tier currency market is to prevent desired capital flows from influencing the exchange rate for current transactions and hence the competitive position of export industries. If the tiering can be policed effectively, a two-tier currency market should protect the exchange rate better than a two-tier credit market. The latter reduces at best the exchange rate impact of investment demand, by allowing the euro-rate to take a greater proportion of strain.

Yet most central banks have resisted the temptations of tiering their exchange market. Tiered credit markets have been preferred to tiered exchange markets by central banks of major currencies. The explanation of the unpopularity of exchange market tiering is to be found first in their international legal complications, and second in difficulties of supervision and administration. Two-tier exchange markets inevitably involve infringements of banking secrecy: the control authority must monitor transactions in order to check whether they were effected in the correct tier.

Can a third tier be avoided?

Two-tier currency markets may generate black markets, where the exchange rate is somewhere between that in the two tiers of the official market. That could occur if residents were not free to export local banknotes, and their import were limited legally.

Belgian control authorities have realized that policing the export or import of franc notes would not be effective. Yet they have tried to ensure that note exports could not lead indirectly to sales of francs in the convertible tier of the exchange market. Their solution has been to allow the free import and export of notes, but subject to the stipulation that franc notes may be debited or credited only to financier franc bank deposits inside Belgium. Thus the Belgian financier franc deposit exchange rate sets boundaries to Belgian franc banknote quotes.

The Belgian solution to the note export problem would be less effective in a country which had a significant surplus on tourist trade with the rest of the world. Then the financial rate would often rise to a premium during the busy tourist season over the commercial rate, and capital exports would be encouraged to a level in excess of what they would be in a unified exchange market.

Two-tier credit markets, in contrast to two-tier exchange markets, do not provide scope for the growth of a third tier of a black credit market, although unofficial leakages will occur inevitably from one tier of the market to the other. The proposition may be well illustrated in the Deutsche mark credit market of the early 1970s. Euro-Deutsche mark bonds then commanded a significant premium over equal maturity domestic German bonds, as the latter could not be sold legitimately by Germans to non-residents. In practice, some leakages occurred: domestic bearer bonds were smuggled to external markets. There, foreigners could acquire them without infringing local regulations. The price of smuggled domestic bonds sold externally approximated to that of euro-Deutsche mark bonds, because buyers could arbitrage freely between the two types. No independent black market in domestic mark bonds could be identified, since, once they had been exported, their prices were almost entirely determined by conditions in the euro-Deutsche mark bond market.

Two-tier market matrix

In figure 4.1, a summary matrix is shown of the different possible combinations of tiering in the exchange and credit market of a given currency. Currencies entered in the first row have unified credit markets, those in the second row have two-tiered credit markets. Currencies entered in the first column have unified exchange markets, those in the second have two-tiered exchange markets.

There is no known example of a currency having both two-tiered

		Exchange Market	
		Unified	Two-Tiered
Credit Market	Unified	US dollar Canadian dollar	Belgian franc
	Two-tiered	Swiss franc	No known example

Figure 4.1 Two-tier Market Matrix

credit and exchange markets. The combination is however theoretically possible. If the Belgo-Luxembourg control authorities restricted non-resident borrowing in the domestic credit market, then a two-tier credit market would be created. During periods of bear pressure on the franc, not only would the financial franc fall to a discount below the convertible, but euro-financier franc interest rates would rise above domestic franc rates. The two-tier credit market would so protect the financier franc from some downward pressure resulting from short-selling by foreigners. In reality, further tiering of the franc markets would narrow them to such an extent as to generate prohibitive transaction costs.

Market re-unification

The larger does the euro-market become relative to the domestic market in the same currency, the less exchange rate effective does the instrument of credit market tiering become. Consider an extreme example. Suppose the euro-Swiss franc market were four times as great as the domestic franc market. Then the exchange rate impact of a given surge in demand for Swiss francs would be little altered by the imposition of a two-tier credit market. Separating off one fifth of the market will not cause euro-franc interest rates to fall much further than they would in a unified market. The incentive to dispense with tiering and its inevitable addition to administrative and transaction costs increases as the euro-market broadens.

In contrast to the Swiss franc, the British pound does not enjoy popularity as a denominator in the euro-markets. Therefore tiering the pound credit market is reasonably effective in reducing pressure on the spot exchange rate from foreign bear selling. So small is the euro-pound money market, that the impact of short-selling there is almost all on the euro-pound interest rate and hardly at all on the spot exchange rate. The euro-pound bond market is narrow. Selling pressure in the euro-pound bond market bears mainly on bond yields rather than on the spot pound exchange rate.

Investment in small euro-bond markets, such as the euro-pound one, that are segmented by controls from their domestic counterparts, is a high risk activity. When the currency is under downward pressure, not only does the exchange rate fall, but bond prices can collapse even when measured in their own unit of account.

LUXEMBOURG AND LICHTENSTEIN

Both Luxembourg and Lichtenstein are independent political jurisdictions within larger currency areas. Luxembourg is an integral part of the Belgo-Luxembourg franc money market. Lichtenstein is placed similarly with respect to the Swiss franc money market. Both situations present interesting loops in the international flow of money.

Luxembourg franc market

Luxembourg banking enjoys the usual privileges that are congenial to the development of an international money market centre; banking secrecy, no reserve requirement, and zero withholding tax. But Luxembourg is more than a euro-market centre. It is an important component of the domestic Belgo-Luxembourg franc market – the Belgian and Luxembourg francs being locked one-to-one in a monetary union. Local Belgo-Luxembourg banks conduct predominantly domestic franc business in the Grand Duchy. Luxembourg is a popular banking centre for Belgians, since interest is paid free of tax there, whilst the Belgian fiscal authorities are not given access to Luxembourg bank records.

Belgian investors in eurobonds make extensive use of Luxembourg's banking facilities, where coupons may be encashed without risk of incurring Belgian tax. An open frontier exists between Belgium and Luxembourg. Since Luxembourg is located within a short distance of most areas of Belgium, bearer bonds can be transmitted there for servicing at costs that are reasonable, even for modest investors.

The Luxembourg franc sector is, in effect, an income tax-free banking zone established within the Belgium-Luxembourg Economic Union. The existence of such a tax-free zone within easy reach of the Belgian population is a possible cause of the Belgian franc's persistent underlying strength, which has so bewildered observers. Whereas tax refuge funds from most countries tend to be invested in currencies other than the country of origin, such funds from Belgium are redeposited largely in Belgo-Luxembourg francs.

Luxembourg is unique among tax havens in forming an integral component of the money market from which a substantial share of its funds come. In other havens, funds tend to be placed in one of the major international currencies – Deutsche marks, US dollars, or Swiss francs.

Figures concerning the exact breakdown of franc business between Belgium and Luxembourg are not available. Evidence of the importance of Luxembourg in the franc money market can be derived from the observation that Brussels money dealers in search of Belgo-Luxembourg francs have a habit of telephoning Luxembourg first. Franc business in Luxembourg is inevitably one-way : banks there have an excess of deposits, since few local outlets are available. Accordingly, the balance is on-lent in the Brussels money market.

Deutsche marks in Luxembourg

At the end of 1977, Luxembourg was the only euromarket centre in which dollars were not the most important sector. The size of the euro-Deutsche mark sector in Luxembourg was greater than it was anywhere else. German bank subsidiaries have formed the heart of Luxembourg Deutsche mark business. The Grand Duchy has been a more popular choice than London from the viewpoint of German head offices: it has the twin advantages of proximity and wide familiarity with the German language. Luxembourg is but a two hours drive from the German financial capital, Frankfurt.

Yet Luxembourg is estranged from the domestic Deutsche mark market. For much of the 1970s, arbitrage between the euro and domestic mark markets was inhibited in various ways, and Luxembourg mark deposit rates have been frequently below domestic mark rates, even for non-bank investors. The German investor seeking a mark tax shelter in Luxembourg has at times had to accept an inferior pre-tax rate of return there.

Luxembourg does not offer low cost tax free deposits to the smaller investor in marks. There is little local retail banking mark business in Luxembourg, as local commerce is conducted in Belgo-Luxembourg francs. Therefore banks are not well placed to act as odd-lot traders in small mark deposits: bid-offer spreads would be high, given the low volume of such business.

Unlike in the Belgian franc sector, in the Deutsche mark sector banknotes cannot be credited at par to Luxembourg bank deposits of the same denomination. If a German arrived with a suitcase of mark banknotes at the counter of a Luxembourg bank and wished to exchange them for a euro-mark deposit, the bank would present him with two choices. First, the bank could charge a transaction cost, based on the estimated charge of shipping the notes to Germany, to be credited to a correspondent account there. Second, the bank could offer to sell Belgo-Luxembourg francs in exchange for the mark notes, credit the francs at par to a bank deposit, which would then be sold in the deposit exchange market for euro-marks. The German would choose the least costly method of exchange. If there was presently a shortage of mark banknotes in Luxembourg, the second route would be chosen. If, instead, the bid price for mark banknotes was equal to the German boundary quote – equal to the bid price for interbank mark deposits less the shipment cost to the German frontier – then it would be cheaper to select the first route.

Banks exchange banknotes for deposits at par only in the local currency. There, the volume of exchange business between bank deposits and notes (in the same denomination) is sufficiently great, and the level of inventories needed for market-making sufficiently low, to justify a zero dealing spread. Only the Belgian investor, therefore, can cart his local banknotes across the Luxembourg frontier, credit a tax free retail deposit there at par, and obtain too an attractive rate.

Swiss francs in Luxembourg

Euro-Swiss franc deposit business is the third major banking activity in Luxembourg, and is entirely wholesale. Euro-franc operations were handicapped increasingly by Swiss National Bank regulations in the late 1970s. The Bank designed certain measures with the objective of adding to the transactions costs of dealing in franc deposits outside Switzerland, and so discouraging growth in the international use of the Swiss money.

Most significantly, Swiss bank head offices are limited in the amount of francs they can sell forward to non-residents. If a euro-bank finds that it has excess euro-franc deposits building up relative to commercial borrowing in francs, it will try to swap these excess francs for dollars by selling them spot for dollars, lending the dollars, and buying francs forward to hedge its exchange positions. The Swiss National Bank's limits on domestic sales of forward francs to foreigners prevent the eurobanks from purchasing francs forward in Switzerland. Instead they must be bought forward from a non-resident bank, which is likely to quote a wider dealing spread, not enjoying the same depth of business in commercial forward franc contracts. The dealing costs on euro-franc deposits are increased by the mentioned difficulties of offsetting inventory in the swap markets.

For short periods, the Swiss National Bank has placed limits on the import of foreign banknotes into Switzerland, hoping thereby to reduce pressure on the franc exchange rate. In practice, the measure has served only to shift some banknote exchange business from Switzerland to other countries. A few investors, in order to avoid bringing in foreign notes, have first sold them for Swiss franc notes in centres such as Luxembourg. Swiss franc notes have so been cross hauled, being dispatched up the Rhine and into the Low Countries, to be sold there to Swiss account investors, who then bring them back to Switzerland. Only by limiting the export of franc notes could the Swiss authorities reduce their purchase by foreigners. Such limits would be in contradiction with the principle of free tradability of the Swiss money.

Lichtenstein loophole

Lichtenstein is part of the Swiss franc area, sharing a common currency with Switzerland, and nominally extending the same controls to non-resident acquisition of francs. However, the Swiss National Bank has not so far had the power to police its controls in Lichtenstein, and the local authorities cannot investigate corporations due to the right of corporate secrecy in the principality. Non-residents of Switzerland have been able to circumvent Swiss controls on foreign purchase of domestic credit instruments by investing through Lichtenstein companies, which have in general enjoyed free access to the domestic Swiss market.

The Swiss National Bank has two possible methods of closing the Lichtenstein loophole. First, it could bring political pressure to bear on Lichtenstein, forcing the principality to revoke the principle of corporate secrecy. That would be against the self-interest of Lichtenstein. Secondly, the Bank could expel Lichtenstein from the Swiss franc area. Lichtenstein residents would be treated as foreigners for the purpose of administration of controls. Swiss franc deposits in Lichtenstein would then have to be lent on, almost entirely, in the euro-Swiss franc rather than the domestic Swiss market. Lichtenstein would so continue to use the Swiss franc as its money, but it would form an integral part of the external rather than internal franc market.

Expulsion from the Swiss franc area would create serious payments problems for Lichtenstein. Most merchandise sold there is bought in Switzerland and domestic Swiss franc transaction balances are needed by Lichtenstein traders to clear payments to Swiss suppliers. Therefore the Swiss National Bank would be likely to set a higher ceiling for the holding of domestic francs by each Lichtenstein resident, than by other non-residents.

Rhine run

Money trading routes, stretching from Rotterdam at one end to Lichtenstein at the other, have been outlined in the present chapter. Nowhere else in the world are so many tradable currencies concentrated within such a small densely populated area. The division of the Rhinelands, the one time kingdom of Lother, between the Dutch guilder, Belgian franc, French franc, Deutsche mark and Swiss franc, has been the basis of development of broad European banknote and external credit markets. Both limit the effective scope of government controls on international trade in their money to a modest amount of exchange and credit market tiering.

5 The Illiquidity Trap

Hell, according to Jean-Paul Sartre, 'c'est les autres.' In his play, 'Huis Clos,' Sartre describes hell as four people locked up in a room together until eternity. In a financial world, Sartre's hell does not depend on a lock and key. Man can be entrapped by illiquidity of personal wealth.

A liquid market is one in which the costs of dealing are low and are hardly reduced by taking time to effect, rather than executing immediately. An illiquid market, in contrast, is one where transaction costs are high and can be reduced substantially by spacing the deal over a period of time.

MARKET LIQUIDITY

Market liquidity can be generated by the services of the auctioneer, or the market-maker, or the broker. All three produce differentiated services, and their costs are distinct functions of market parameters such as turnover rate and price volatility of the commodity traded. The *market-maker* offers the service of providing a continuous two-way market. The *auctioneer* is skilled in mustering a wide group of potential buyers for a commodity which is to be sold. The *broker* seeks to identify two parties who want to deal in opposite directions in the same commodity.

Grading market liquidity

Markets may be graded from the most illiquid in which only brokerage is found, to the most liquid in which brokerage, auctioneering, and market-making are all to be found (see figure 5.1). The comparative costs of market-making and auctioneering are so great in certain markets, that participants choose always the liquidity services of the broker.

Markets in which
Liquidity Services Provided by:

(1)	(2)	(3)
brokers only	brokers and auctioneers	brokers, auctioneers and market-makers
secondary real estate, unquoted securities	prime real estate, master art works	money, commodities, foreign exchange, quoted securities, rare books, stamps, art

Figure 5.1 Grading Market Liquidity

Neither auctioneers nor market-makers are to be found usually for unquoted securities of private corporations. Auctioneering would be expensive, because the corporation is unlikely to be known to many of the potential purchasers, and it would take a long time and much effort to muster sufficient numbers for an auction. Market-makers could not function economically, due to the non-standardization of product, low volume of buyers and sellers, and price risk of the commodity (see following section).

The Mona Lisa is a highly liquid commodity. The Louvre need only advertise its sale at a forthcoming auction in one month's time, and the gallery would be assured of a full auction hall! So well known is the work, and so wide the purchasing interest, that little effort is required to bring the Mona Lisa market into existence.

The Mona Lisa is a unique product. Only where a high volume of purchases and sales occurs can a continuous market be maintained, via the operations of a market-maker. Hence the market-maker is found in high turnover markets such as those for money, commodities, foreign exchange, and quoted securities. Elsewhere, the would-be transactor must incur the costs of calling a market into existence.

The market-maker

Market-making is a risky business. The market-maker stands ready to deal instantaneously at his bid and offer rates. Until he manages to offset the deal in the opposite direction he sustains an inventory risk.

Consider a market-maker in spot Deutsche marks against US dollars, whose initial quote is 1.8650–60 Dm $ Suppose he is offered marks for dollars at 1.8660 Dm/$. He hopes very quickly to be bid for Deutsche marks against dollars by another customer at 1.8650 Dm/$. His dealing turn is uncertain: the mark may have slipped in the interval to 1.8670–80 Dm/$. The market-maker's profit is the cumulative difference between the cost of Deutsche marks purchased and the sale values realized.

Is the bearing of risk, as measured above, a service for which the market-maker deserves to earn a return? It could be argued that on average losses and gains should cancel out, and that the market-maker is in reality exposed to zero risk. Further, if inventory positions are maintained overnight, the market-maker will earn interest income equal to the expected movement of one currency against the other.

Both arguments fail to acknowledge key aspects of the market-making function. First, the market-maker cannot hold continuously a well-diversified portfolio. His dealing activity will require at times substantial swings from the optimum distribution of risk assets. Second, the market-maker is not an ordinary investor, who chooses securities as a price-taker. The market-maker is *making* his price, and he must make it *continuously*.

The function of providing continuous liquidity inevitably involves 'leaning against the wind.' In the early stages of what turns out to be a speculative wave of selling, the market-maker will find himself at first buying for inventory, and conversely. He will not speculate ordinarily whether the early ebb of selling is but a prelude to a larger wave: he must maintain a two-way market. If the market-maker tried to out-guess the market and hoped to anticipate speculative waves by moving his bid and offer quotes in their direction, he would himself become a major speculator in the market. He would change his quotes in a discontinuous fashion, and deal in one direction only for most of the time. Risk considerations would limit the volume of this one-way trading. He would be unable to attain the high volume turnover figures and the low ratio of inventory to turnover of the successful market-maker, who could thereby quote lower dealing spreads.

If, alternatively, the market-maker widened his bid-offer spread every time he feared a change in the direction of speculative operations, he would become known as a 'fair weather market-maker' who closed up shop whenever conditions became difficult. He would not succeed in building up a large clientele. Market participants, for reasons of information gathering costs, including mutual credit rating assessment, tend to group into reasonably steady clienteles of different market-makers.

Determining the bid-offer spread

The size of bid-offer spread quoted by a market-maker has three major determinants. The first two, price volatility per unit period of the commodity traded, and the average holding period of inventory, have been described briefly in chapter 2. The less frequent are transactions in a commodity, the greater is the danger that a substantial change in speculative tide can occur without being registered in many transactions and being recognized by each market-maker. The third determinant of bid-offer spread is inventory storage costs. The higher are such costs (including insurance and loss of interest), the greater will be the dealing spread, unless such costs are discounted already in the spot price, as for pure investment commodities such as gold.

Collusion between dealers

Market-makers may collude, albeit illegally, to fix a common range of quote. Protection may be gained thereby against the risk of large losses from 'leaning against the wind.' For example, the major banks in a centre may fear that panic selling of the dollar is about to occur. Rather than each acting severally, and reducing their dollar quotes gradually, they together anticipate the speculative tide by marking down immediately their dollar quotes by a large margin. The conspirators market-make continuously, and their dealing income is not threatened by their combined speculative action. If in contrast, an individual market-maker acted alone as a speculator by lowering his quote, his dealing turnover would suffer as he tended to deal in one direction only. He would develop a large speculative position.

Inter-market-maker dealing

A property which appears general to all markets in which market-makers are found – whether in art, stamps, or financial instruments – is the large volume of inter-market-maker business. The motivation of such business is the minimization of risk. In a market in which there are many dealers (i.e. market-makers), they will find themselves very often with offsetting positions. In the Deutsche mark-US dollar example, some dealers will find often an excess of marks building up simultaneously with another finding himself with an excess of dollars against marks. Such offsetting positions arise because of the stochastic fashion in which business comes to individual market-makers. Aggregate risk in the market-making industry, and consequently the level of bid-offer spreads, is reduced if off-setting positions are cleared quickly by an inter-dealer transaction.

If an individual market-maker, Mr. Ego, pursued a policy of never dealing with other market-makers, he would find that his ratio of turnover to inventory was abnormally low, and hence his bid-offer spread would be uncompetitive. Equivalently, Mr. Ego would find that the average holding period of his inventory would be reduced by being willing to offload inventory onto other dealers who had been 'hit' by non-dealer demand in the opposite direction.

If no inter-market-maker transacting occurred, and each dealer ran an independent inventory, the ratio of aggregate inventories to turnover would be abnormally high, as would be spreads. Any two dealers would find that they could quote more competitively by amalgamating their operations. And so the trend would become apparent towards general amalgamation of independent market-makers.

Where inter-market-maker activity occurs, and the costs are negligible of inter-dealer negotiation, including information gathering costs such as brokerage fees, the number of dealers would indeed be irrelevant to the observed size of bid-offer spreads. The typical bid-offer spread in each commodity would be determined simply by the total non-dealer turnover rate in the commodity, and other parameters described already. Each dealer would be effectively a branch outlet of a central market-making function. In practice, brokerage fees in interbank business are significant, so that bid-offer spreads in a commodity are not independent of the number of market-makers.

A snapshot taken of sample quotes in Deutsche marks against US dollars of competing market-makers would show them all to be different. The differences between the largest and smallest bid price, and between the largest and smallest offer price, will be less than or equal to the typical bid-offer spread, thus eliminating the possibility of pure arbitrage operations by non-dealers. Inter-dealer transacting is triggered as soon as one dealer's bid quote rises to another's offer quote, or conversely. Suppose that Dealer One finds excess inventory of marks building up relative to dollars, and conversely for Dealer Two. Dealer One reduces his quote for marks, and Dealer Two raises his. When Dealer One's offer rate for marks comes to equal Dealer Two's bid rate, as for example when Dealer One quotes 1.8060–70 Dm/$ and Dealer Two quotes 1.8050–60 Dm/$, the two transact with each other. Dealer One sheds marks to Dealer Two in exchange for dollars. The trigger-point is altered slightly when information gathering costs are substantial.

Choice between liquidity services

In some markets, all three types of liquidity service are provided, and the transactor will choose one consistent with his own particular needs. If the market-maker is selected, greatest importance is being attached probably to dealing immediately rather than to the minimization of transaction cost. If the broker is selected, with instruction to match the order directly with another client, transaction cost should be least. But the risks of broker dishonesty and of greater delay are incurred. If a large volume is to be dealt in, the use of an auctioneer is normally most appropriate: indeed, in some equity markets it is legally necessary. Market-makers' limited capacity to absorb inventory make them ill-suited to effect huge transactions.

An example of a market in which there are brokers, auctioneers, and market-makers is that in the French franc. At midday, each trading day, a five-minute 'fixing' occurs for the French franc on the Paris Bourse. 'Fixing' is in reality an auction, at which foreign currencies are sold for francs. The Bank of France acts as auctioneer. Transactors who do not believe that they can spot a particularly good dealing opportunity during the morning can generally save on transaction costs by requesting their bank to effect the deal at the official fixing price. An individual bank matches such orders from many clients and deals on a net basis at the fix. It assumes some dealing risk because the price actually realized may differ from the official fixing price, which is the clearing price determined by the auctioneer after a short period of concentrated trading, during which the bulk of business occurs at different prices. The saving in transaction costs is achieved by the bank being able to match orders prior to the fix, and by the high volume of turnover at the fix.

The Italian lira exchange market features a midday 'fixing' session in Rome. Here the Banca d'Italia actually fixes the price, rather than acting as auctioneer. Having been informed first of the net orders of each major bank, the Bank then announces the fixing rate at which it is unreservedly prepared to do business. Any net sales (or purchases) are absorbed by the Bank itself. Transactors must choose between using their own bank as broker to the Banca d'Italia, or transacting outside fixing time.

When market-makers vanish

During volatile trading conditions, market-makers may decide to shut up shop. The wide bid-offer spread, that they would quote to compensate for the great inventory risk assumed, would outprice their services relative to those of the broker and auctioneer for almost all transactors.

One example of market-making eclipse was during the dollar crisis in November 1978. On November 2, the US government announced a package of measures designed to rally the dollar. For the rest of that afternoon dealing spreads in the exchange markets were over two per cent, as market-makers were faced with the uncertainty of how, on reflection, the measures would be interpreted. Transactors switched to leaving limit orders with their bank which would be matched when someone wishing to deal in the opposite direction within the set price range could be found: continuous liquidity was no longer available in practice.

Market-making can evaporate for more lengthy periods in markets where the commodity traded cannot easily be short-sold. For example, leaning against a speculative wind of purchases of spot copper will tend to leave market-makers in the metal with abnormally low inventory. Unlike in money, or freely tradable currency markets, market-makers will find it difficult to borrow the spot commodity. Thus during periods of run-down inventories, some market-makers will cease operations, while others will quote abnormally high spreads. Purchasers of material tend to switch to buying from suppliers direct, or at auction, rather than from market-makers on the floor of a commodity exchange.

DIVERSIFICATION IN MARKET-MAKING

It is rare for a dealer to market-make in only one commodity. In the exchange market, a bank will trade typically at least two or three currencies: in the metal markets, a dealer will market-make often in both silver and gold, or copper and zinc. These findings are explained by the properties of risk diversification.

Zonal groups

In the first two chapters, it was shown how certain commodities could be identified as belonging to zones, whose prices over short intervals are particularly closely correlated. Market-making in different commodities belonging to the same zone is often complimentary.

Consider the example of Dutch guilders and Deutsche marks, where changes in the guilder-dollar and mark-dollar exchange rates are highly correlated. The market-maker, Mr. Duo, who deals in both marks and guilders against dollars, enjoys an advantage compared to Mr. Uno, who deals in only guilders against dollars, when quoting for guilder-dollar business. If Mr. Duo finds that he has excess guilder inventory building up against dollars, he can reduce not only the dollar price of guilders but also of marks and hope to reduce more quickly his exposure to trans-zonal exchange risk than would Mr. Uno in similar circumstances. Trans-zonal risk of either the guilder or mark against the dollar is considerably greater than the intra-zonal risk of the guilder against the mark. Mr. Duo has greater scope than Mr. Uno to transform trans-zonal into intra-zonal positions, which are lower risk, hoping to reverse the latter in due course.

Mr. Duo, by market-making in several mark zone currencies against the dollar, should be able to increase his trans-zonal inventory turnover rate, where inventory is regarded as homogeneous within the same zone. How far such consolidation of trans-zonal inventory permits a reduction of bid-offer spreads in each currency against the dollar depends on how much greater is trans-zonal than intra-zonal risk.

Mr. Duo, on finding an excess build-up of guilder inventory against dollars, should not reduce both his guilder and mark quotes equiproportionately. He cannot differentiate immediately whether the excess guilders are simply the early rain drops of a general switch out of mark zone currencies into the dollar, or a localized fall confined to the Dutch exchange market. Therefore Mr. Duo reduces at first his guilder quote by more than that of other mark zone currencies. If he soon becomes convinced that the guilder sales were raindrops preluding a general trans-zonal storm, then he would mark down other mark zone currencies to a similar extent to the guilder.

Banks, small and large

The experience of Mr. Duo in the above example explains both why market-makers specialize rarely in one commodity, and why certain financial centres, such as Zurich and London, have grown to trade many third country currencies against the US dollar. A Zurich bank, by trading many European currencies, not just the Swiss franc, against the dollar, can increase significantly its turnover rate in the dollar against mark zone currencies. The same incentive towards extending the range of currencies traded does not exist for banks (such as German ones) whose 'natural' foreign exchange business is already in a large, high turnover currency.

Large, well capitalized banks are equipped to market-make in many currencies. Like in other industries, in foreign exchange dealing small firms have to specialize to a greater extent than large enterprises. The area of specialization should be chosen carefully. The small bank has maximum comparative advantage in market-making in European currencies which are independent of, or on the outside of the Deutsche mark zone, and hence where least advantage is gained from currency diversification. The small bank has also a comparative advantage in trading the Canadian dollar against the US dollar, because the Canadian dollar-US dollar exchange rate is little correlated with European currency-dollar exchange rates.

Diversification across dates

The principle of diversification in market-making may be extended to trading different dates in the same commodity. For example, the spot, three, six, and twelve-month rates of the Deutsche mark against the US dollar are all highly correlated. Banks treat spot exchange and outright forwards as merely differentiated branches of basic Deutsche mark-US dollar exchange business, and measure their dollar-mark inventory by netting exchange exposure across all forward and spot dates combined. On a secondary level, it manages its exposure to spot-against-forward (swap) risk. If a bank finds excess inventory of Deutsche mark outright forwards developing, whilst spot inventory is meanwhile in balance, it would reduce both its spot and forward quotes for the mark. As in the earlier guilder-mark example, the bank would reduce the forward quote by more than the spot one, being unable at first to ascertain whether selling of the forward mark was localized, or a prelude to generalized selling of marks across all dates.

Speculative positions for or against a currency are assumed to a greater extent in each of the one, two, and three-month forward markets than in the spot or more distant forward markets. A high proportion of exchange speculation assumes the form of deciding whether or not to hedge forward commitments, which tend to be concentrated in the ranges mentioned. The impact of a change in speculative opinion appears so to be greater on forward than on spot exchange rates. When sentiment becomes more bullish towards the guilder, say, its forward premium against the dollar reacts upwards. Speculation in the spot market impacts directly on the guilder credit market, as purchasers of guilders must intend simultaneously to lend them there. The reaction of interest rates increases with the size of the guilder exchange relative to the guilder credit market.

The speculative impact described on the credit and exchange markets will create an arbitrage opportunity exploitable by borrowing dollars to invest in guilders and buying dollars forward. The opportunity will be greatest when the interest rate adjustment to spot speculation is smallest, as for currencies of large countries. The extent to which the arbitrage gap is closed by interest rate falls in the credit market compared to a fall of the dollar against the guilder in the spot market depends on how market-makers in each react to perceived excess inventory build-up. The smaller is the credit market relative to the exchange markets, the greater will be the adjustment of interest rates relative to the spot rate.

If the central bank, however, pursues a policy of pegging nominal short-term guilder interest rates, rather than allowing them to be determined freely and setting monetary growth independently, greater pressure will be borne by the spot rate. The dangers of fixing interest rates, rather than setting money supply targets, however, are becoming increasingly well-known.

Calm before the storm

Speculation in interest rate futures, in contrast to currency futures, can cause spot rates to move in opposite direction to that of expectations about future rates. For example, a feared tightening of monetary policy within three months would stimulate borrowers to raise long maturity finance, whilst lenders would try to shorten the maturity of their loans in anticipation of a rising interest rate. Such speculative operations cause increased demand for three-month and longer credit, and increased supply of less than three-month maturity credit. Expectations of an upward shift in the cost of short-term borrowing so reduce its present cost whilst increasing that of longer term borrowing. The sharpness of the eventual rise in short-term rates is increased, albeit from a lowered base.

Speculation in interest rate futures can be analogous in some respects to speculation in futures markets of currencies whose spot exchange rate is pegged by central bank intervention. The analogy holds when the central bank operates an adjustable peg system for short-term interest rates in their domestic money market. Forward interest rates float freely.

Suppose the demand for credit of both short and long maturity surges. Further, the central bank injects monetary base into the short-term bill market to maintain its interest rate peg there. Expectations would prevail that the peg was inconsistent with money supply targets, and that the short-term interest rate would soon be adjusted upwards. Speculative pressure in the forward T-Bill market would cause the one-month forward T-Bill rate, say, to be at a large premium over the spot rate. Spot market intervention so increases volatility of forward-forward rates (see *Money, Hard and Soft*, pp. 111–12). The speculator who believes that soon the market will revise upwards its expected rate of rise of interest rates would buy 3-month T-Bills forward one month and simultaneously sell them forward three months. He would hope to profit as the yield curve steepened, on his belief being proved correct.

If the central bank set simply a target for high-powered money supply growth and allowed interest rates to float freely, short-term interest rates would become more volatile over short periods of time. Supply and demand for short maturity credit are inelastic, as spending, investment, and inventory decisions cannot be altered quickly in response to changing credit costs. On impact, an upward shift in demand for credit of all maturities would cause very short-term rates to rise sharpest. Subsequently these would fall back, and the yield curve would tend to flatten albeit at a higher level than prior to the demand shift.

Analogously, in foreign exchange markets, elasticity of substitution between near-term forward and spot exchange with respect to the forward premium over spot is small. Trading plans can be changed only slowly and flexibility of payment dates is limited. Considerable volatility of near-term forward premia is likely where they are not pegged directly or indirectly by central bank operations. The source of volatility is uneven influence of speculation on spot and forward rates.

Despite the many similarities that exist between speculating on interest rates and exchange rates, there are some important differences. In *Money, Hard and Soft*, I distinguished first and second order speculation, which involve smoothing out price fluctuations in the spot market, from third order speculation which changes the relation of futures prices to each other. First and second order speculation is more limited in credit than currency markets. All participants may expect interest rates to rise sharply after one year, yet that could be consistent with their marginal time preferences for consumption now and in future periods, and no speculative opportunity would be present. Such speculation would assume the form of increasing present consumption, and intending to save more intensively when interest rates rise.

The overnight interest rate, in contrast to the spot exchange rate, is a non-speculative variable. Speculative positions cannot be assumed overnight in one-day deposits, because they age into sight deposits by the following morning. Direct speculation cannot link, therefore, overnight interest rates from day to day, and large inter-temporal fluctuations are possible.

Swap markets

In addition to dealing in outright spot and forward commodities, market-makers deal also in swaps. Swaps involve the exchange of a commodity spot for the same commodity at a future date. Buying marks for dollars spot, and selling simultaneously marks for dollars three months forward is an example of a dollar for mark swap.

Swap transactions have two main sources. First, commercial hedgers when they roll-over forward contracts at maturity effect swap deals. Second, market-makers in spot and outright forwards initiate swap transactions often with each other. The volume of non-dealer swap transactions is much lower than that of non-dealer spot business. Hence there tend to be fewer market-makers in swap than in outright exchange. Many independent market-makers in outright exchange will off-load their swap exposures on to the smaller number of market-makers in swaps. Thus a high proportion of inter-market-maker business, particularly in foreign exchange, is in swaps.

Bid-offer spreads are usually very narrow in swaps, because the price volatility per unit period of swap margins is low. In most commodity and money markets spot and forward prices are highly correlated, so that the difference between them is much less volatile than for either by itself.

SATELLITE MARKET FORMATIONS

A market-maker makes a market in commodity A against B only if it is cheaper to do so than to combine quotes from markets for A against C and B against C. Whether a narrower bid-offer spread can be so formed from dealing in A directly against B, or as satellite to A and B against C, depends on the comparative business turnover in the three exchanges and the comparative price volatilities per unit period of A/B, A/C, and B/C. In subsequent sections, concrete examples are drawn of this abstract formulation.

Spot foreign exchange

Most spot exchange transactions are effected through the dollar vehicle. The volume of non-bank transactions is so much greater in British pounds and Deutsche marks against US dollars than in British pounds against Deutsche marks, that it is cheaper to form mark-pound quotes by combining a mark-dollar and dollar-pound quote than by quoting direct (see *Money, Hard and Soft*, pp. 43–5).

In almost all currency markets the volume of non-bank transactions against the dollar is greater than against any other currency. Such dollar pre-eminence is explained by first, the dollar being a widely used numeraire in commodity markets (in particular for oil), second, the large share of the US in trade, and third, the large volume of international borrowing and lending in the dollar. As discussed in chapters 2 and 3, growth of monetary co-ordination in Europe could cause the dollar to be replaced by the mark as numeraire in world commodity trade. Then the volume inequalities that promote the dollar's vehicle property in exchange markets could be reversed.

Even if the dollar remained pre-eminent as numeraire in world trade, the mark could achieve a limited vehicle status. Suppose zonal relationships in Western Europe were to increase in force, and the short-term volatility of the French franc-Deutsche mark rate were less than that of the French franc-dollar. Then a bank market-making in French francs against Deutsche marks direct should be able to quote a lower bid-offer spread than by intending to offset in the Deutsche mark-dollar and French franc-dollar markets. Although business turnover in francs against marks would be less than in the two dollar exchange markets, the price risk per unit inventory in franc-marks would be relatively low.

Small independent spot markets

Independent markets do exist for small size transactions, but not for large, between certain non-dollar currencies. For example, Dutch banks make a market directly between guilders and marks for small size transactions. Yet large guilder-mark transactions are effected almost entirely through the dollar.

The observance of different practices for dealing in large and small amounts suggests that the cost of market-making decreases at a diminishing rate as business turnover rates increase. That could be explained by the turnover rate of inventory increasing at a diminishing rate as turnover increases, which is a familiar property in inventory analysis. In large size transactions the volume of deals is low and the greater business in marks-dollars and guilders-dollars than in marks-guilders makes market-making directly in marks against guilders uneconomical. In the range of small size transactions the volume of deals is large: there volume differences are less important, and price volatility per unit inventory more important as a determinant of market-making practice. The relation of transaction cost to volume in each market so explains why independent market-making in guilders-marks prevails for small transactions.

The Dutch gold bullion market provides another example of market-maker independence of the dollar for small size transactions. Banks in the Netherlands will quote for small deals narrower spreads on gold against guilders than the combination of spreads on gold against dollars and dollars against guilders. Independence might survive even if the volatility of the gold-guilder exchange rate were greater than that of the gold-dollar rate, because the costs of maintaining two dealing inventories would be avoided. However, the smaller is turnover in guilders-gold relative to gold-dollars and dollar-guilders, the more likely it is that indirect quotation would prove cheaper in guilder-gold, even for small size transactions.

Satellite forward quotation

In foreign exchange markets, outright forward quotes are made often on a satellite basis to the swap and spot markets. The practice can be explained by the observation that business in any particular forward date, say three months, is less than in spot exchange. Often non-bank business in swaps is higher volume than in outright forwards, and the price volatility of swap inventory is much lower than that of outright exchange inventory. So by combining deals in the high volume spot exchange market with the low risk swap market, it may be possible for a market-maker to quote more cheaply than by market-making directly in outright forwards.

An example of satellite formation of outright forward quotes is provided in figure 5.2. The spread on the three-month outright forward quote is shown there to be the sum of those on spot and three-month swap deals.

spot Dm/$	1.8788–98
3-month swap	250–245
3-month outright forward Dm $	1.8538–1.8553

Figure 5.2 Satellite outright forward quotation

Sometimes outright forward exchange quotation is direct. That occurs when either the volume of non-dealer business in outright forward exchange is particularly high, or the volatility of swap margins is close to the volatility of outright forward rates.

In a very open economy, non-dealer business turnover in outright forwards, which arises mainly from trade hedging, may be higher relative to that in swaps than for a more closed economy. Commercial business in swaps originates more from investment hedging and less from trade hedging than that in outright forwards. If three months is the most frequent hedging period, then it is possible that independent market-making will occur in outright three-month forwards.

Swap margins between small currencies, or currencies of restricted tradability, and the US dollar tend to be particularly volatile. In both types of currency, swap margins adjust more and spot exchange rates less in response to changing expectations about future spot exchange rates than do those in large fully convertible currencies (see *Money, Hard and Soft*, pp. 13–18). In small freely tradable currencies, the credit market is small relative to the exchange market and speculative flows can cause sharp interest rate movements. In restricted currencies, forward rates have a weak tie to the spot rate, because covered arbitrage flows are constrained. Volatile swap margins increase the chances that direct market-making will prevail in outright forwards.

Official intervention to peg the spot exchange rate against one currency or a basket of currencies results in increased volatility of the swap margin. The forward exchange rate, unlike the spot rate, is unprotected against speculative onslaughts. When the British pound was pegged to the US dollar in the early part of 1977, pound interest rates and the pound-dollar swap margin became abnormally volatile. Outright forward exchange dealing in three-month pounds became commonplace, as the combined spread on three-month swap and spot deals came to exceed the level at which direct market-making in three-month forwards could be profitable for banks.

Where official intervention is designed to peg a currency to a weighted basket of currencies rather than to one currency, the cost of manufacturing outright forward rates on a satellite basis to the swap and spot markets is likely to be higher than directly. Exchange markets do not exist for currencies against baskets. The bid-offer spread in the spot market for dollars against pounds would be higher if the pound was pegged against the SDR than against the US dollar. The SDR peg implies higher volatility of the spot dollar-pound rate than a dollar peg. Thus official intervention to peg the domestic currency against a weighted basket, coupled with either restrictions on arbitrage or a small domestic credit base, would provide greenhouse conditions for independent market-making in outright forward exchange.

Illustrations of possible satellite relationships in forward markets are found in figure 5.3. The Chicago IMM and commodity market examples are discussed in subsequent sections.

Market-making in distant forwards

In some markets, forward trading extends into maturities as far distant as eighteen months. Both the dispersion in volume of trading between forward dates and the volatility of the forward-forward rates between dates varies considerably in different markets (see table 5.1). Such nonuniformity helps explain different market-making practices found in long maturity forward markets which are summarized in figure 5.4.

Forward-forward rates are the difference between forward rates for the same commodity for different dates. Thus, if a dealer quotes 225–215 for three-month Deutsche marks against six-month Deutsche marks, both against the US dollar, that means he would sell marks for dollars in three months at a 215 point discount below what he would simultaneously agree to buy them back at in six months' time: he would sell dollars for marks in three months at a 225 point premium above the rate at which he would agree simultaneously to buy them back in six months' time.

Forward-forward rates are most volatile in small currencies, restricted currency, and non-investment commodity markets. The first two examples were demonstrated in the previous section. The third depends on arbitrage properties between commodity futures and money markets. An investment commodity is defined as one in which present stocks are large relative to commercial demand, and so a large proportion is held by investors who derive no convenience yield. In such commodities, the ratio of forward premium to spot price must equal the local money interest rate plus storage costs. Hence forward-forward

	spot	swap	forward-forward	3-month outright forward
interbank $-Dm	prime	prime	satellite to swap market	satellite to swap and spot markets
Chicago IMM $-Dm	satellite to inter-bank $-Dm	prime	prime	prime
interbank Italian lira-$	prime	prime	satellite to swap market	prime
interbank Mexican pesos-$	prime	prime	satellite to Chicago IMM forward-forward market	prime
interbank $-£ when spot rate pegged to $	market made by Bank of England	prime	satellite to swap market	prime
interbank $-£ when spot rate floating	prime	prime	satellite to swap market	satellite to swap and spot markets
copper on Comex NY	satellite to swap and out-right forward market	prime	prime	prime

Figure 5.3 Market-making in spot, swap, forward-forward and outright forward markets

rates approximate the forward interest rate for the period between the same two forward dates. For non-investment commodities forward-forward rates can be highly variable. If, for example, a shortage occurs in near term sugar supplies, yet large inward shipments are expected in three months time, the three-month price could fall to a large discount below the spot price, or one-month price. The forward-forward rates of non-investment commodities are not bounded below, and can sky-rocket during periods of present famine.

Table 5.1 Open interest by maturity
November 15, 1978

1. *copper* (Comex)		2. *gold* (IMM)		3. *silver* (Chicago Board of Trade)	
Dec	12,209	Dec	12,548	Dec	10,359
Mar 79	21,613	Mar	21,910	Feb	29,439
May	8,483	June	24,630	Apr	50,221
July	6,196	Sept	19,530	June	41,534
Sept	3,201	Dec	9,284	Aug	40,338
Dec	4,949	Mar	4,472	Oct	24,369
		June	1,964	Dec	16,474
				Feb	10,173

4. *sugar* (CSE)		5. *T-Bills* (IMM)	
Jan 79	203	Dec	3,165
Mar	16,644	Mar 79	7,207
May	5,253	June	7,692
July	3,344	Sept	7,525
Sept	2,000	Dec	8,608
Oct	2,536	Mar	6,827
Jan	3	June	5,252
		Sept	2,633

Source: Wall Street Journal

Sugar is an example of a non-investment commodity. Although the volume of trading is highly concentrated in the three-month forward date (see table 5.1), other dates are not satellite to the three-month market. The bid-offer spread on sugar forward-forward quotes for three against six months is wide, due to their volatility. It is therefore cheapest to market-make in six-month sugar directly, while benefiting from the principle of diversification across highly correlated prices, already discussed.

In the Chicago Board of Trade silver market, volume is divided fairly evenly between future dates up to six months ahead. Dealers will make a market directly in maturities up to six months, and sometimes nine months. Beyond that, market-making is satellite to shorter dated forwards and the spread (forward-forward) market. Not only are spreads low risk, but a high volume of non-dealer business is transacted in them. Such business is largely composed of tax spreads: by buying silver six months forward, and selling twelve months forward, the tax payer is exposed to little risk. Yet the volatility of the price of silver is high, and the tax payer has a good opportunity of being able to realize a loss on one leg of the transaction, which can be used to reduce income

	3-month	6-month	12-month
IMM $-Dm	prime	satellite to 3-month and 3-to-6 month forward-forward markets	satellite to 3-month and interbank swap markets
interbank $-Dm	satellite to spot and swap markets	satellite to spot and swap markets	satellite to spot, euro-Dm, and euro-$ markets
interbank $-French franc	prime	prime	prime
IMM gold	prime	prime	prime
LME copper	prime	satellite to 3-month and deposit markets	satellite to 3-month and deposit markets
Comex copper	prime	satellite to 3-month and 3-to-6 month forward-forward markets	satellite to 3-month and 3-to-12 month forward-forward markets
Chicago B of T silver	prime	prime	satellite to 3-month and 3-to-12 month forward-forward markets
Sugar CSE	prime	prime	prime
IMM-T-Bills	prime	satellite to 3-month and 3-to-6 month forward-forward markets	satellite to 3-month and 3-to-12 month forward-forward markets

Figure 5.4 Market-making practices in near and distant forwards

tax liabilities arising elsewhere.

The high volume of trading in spreads and their low risk implies that bid-offer spreads on silver forward-forward deals are very low. Hence, as trading volume shrinks beyond nine months, satellite quotation of forwards predominates.

Mathematical inequalities between turnover rates and risk of spreads compared with outright forwards are not an infallible guide to whether distant forward quotes will be satellite in nature. Distant forward quotes in gold are made independently on Chicago's International Monetary Market (IMM) by market-makers who do not deal in swaps, despite gold sharing the investment qualities and tax spread business of silver. However, the trading floor for gold is cramped, and the different dates and spreads are traded on different levels of the pit. Given the high volume of noise and activity, there are high 'transaction costs' involved in the distant forward trader operating on a satellite basis to near forward and forward-forward traders.

In the Chicago IMM T-Bill futures market, trading volume is fairly even for dates up to almost a year ahead. Yet forward-forward trading is normally lower risk there than in the silver and gold markets. The difference between the three-month and six-month T-Bill futures rates is the forward yield differential between six-month and three-month T-Bills in three months time. This differential is considerably less volatile than the three-month T-Bill rate itself, except over very short periods. The lower volatility itself encourages a high volume of tax spreading business. Both features act to reduce the transaction costs of forward-forward business in T-Bills, and only quotes for the three-month forward date are made independently.

Satellite swap markets

Dealers are able to quote for swap business on a satellite basis to other markets. A bank which quotes for selling marks against dollars spot to buy back forward in three months can offset the resulting swap exposure by intending to borrow marks for three months and investing in a three-month dollar deposit. Whether it chooses to operate so, as a satellite to the dollar and mark deposit markets, or to make a direct market in swaps, depends on a comparison of risk and turnover rates in the respective markets. Though direct market-making in swaps is most common, in two situations, satellite quotation will prevail.

First, volume of business in swaps may be very low relative to that in the respective deposit markets. Then the combination of bid-offer spreads from the two deposit markets would be less than the spread at which it would be economical to run an inventory in swaps direct. Such inequality of turnover is found often for long-dated swaps, as exchange market turnover slows more rapidly than deposit market turnover when maturities lengthen.

Second, the volatility of the swap rate (or equivalently, the interest rate differential between the two currency brands of deposit) may be considerably larger than that of the interest rate in either deposit market. That could occur during a period of wide fluctuations of the mark-dollar axis, when interest rates on marks and dollars tend to move in opposite direction. During 1977–8, a period of mark-dollar crisis, banks often made markets in swaps on a satellite basis to the deposit markets.

Flexible approach to market-making

The choice between satellite and independent market-making is determined by a comparison of turnover rates and price change volatilities in the candidate component markets. Niether volatility nor turnover statistics are constant, and it should not be expected that market-making practices will remain standard at all times.

During periods of rapid shifts in taste between the two major international monies, dollars and marks, trans-zonal volatility of exchange rates increases relative to intra-zonal volatility. It may then become possible to quote a lower spread on Deutsche marks against French francs direct, than combining a franc-dollar and mark-dollar quote. Indeed the same principle may apply to more distant zonal members, such as the British pound.

CHICAGO BULLS

Bulls on the Chicago International Monetary Market (IMM) believe that the IMM could one day account for a major share of the US foreign exchange market. Opponents of the new market consider the IMM to be no more than a speculative fringe market with no great potential. Analysis of the market within the context of the structure of market-making described here suggests that the IMM has a comparative advantage in certain type of markets, many of which have not yet been developed.

IMM comparative advantages

The IMM will never be able to compete with banks in making a market for spot exchange. In the spot market, payments are effected within two days, and futures markets are ill-equipped to handle such transactions. Their method of assuring payment, the placing of margins, is not workable for spot deals.

Yet market-making in forward exchange is complimentary to spot exchange, and often satellite to it. Thus the IMM's comparative advantage should be in currencies for which the economies from dealing in spot and forward exchange together are least. Currencies with volatile swap and forward-forward rates so suggest themselves, the Italian lira or Mexican peso for example.

Further, volatile swap and forward-forward rates encourage speculative business in trading one future date against another. The IMM organization, based on that of commodity futures markets, is more suited than the interbank to forward-forward trades between dates, and market-making in these occurs directly. A large volume of forward-forward business (commonly called 'spread' business in Chicago) adds to the liquidity of the outright forward markets, by increasing the opportunities for satellite formation of quotes when trading in one date is particularly low volume. Unlike in the silver and gold futures markets, tax spreading is not common in IMM currency markets. The risk of spreads on currencies is often greater, and the volatility of the outright forwards less than in the gold and silver markets, a combination ill-suited to effective tax spreading.

The Italian lira and Mexican peso are both examples of currencies in which arbitrage between the forward exchange and domestic credit markets is restricted, whereby swap and spread rates are volatile. The Mexican peso has been one of the IMM's most successful contracts, and the IMM accounts for the major share of forward business in the total peso market, far ahead of the IMM's share in any other market. The Mexican peso example suggests that the IMM may score similar advantage in the Australian dollar, where the spot rate is pegged, and both forward and swap rates potentially volatile.

The Italian lira futures contract when introduced originally on the IMM was a failure. A number of explanations are suggested. First, economic statistics are late and unreliable for Italy, which retards developments of speculative interest in trading. Second, IMM lira trading ceased when the lira market became two-tiered in the mid-1970s. The organisers of the IMM are opposed to the trading of two-tiered currencies on the exchange. If the commercial tier is traded delivery problems arise because official documentation is required before convertible currency (lira) could be delivered to fulfil a contract. There is not much interest in trading financial tier currency, as trade hedgers deal in the convertible tier.

The two-tiered nature of the Belgian franc exchange market has prevented the introduction of a Belgian franc contract on to the IMM.

Besides delivery problems, exchange officials regard both markets as too narrow, and too tightly controlled by the concentrated Belgian banking industry, to provide an entry opportunity for outside competitors. The Belgian franc is hardly traded in New York after Europe closes, and arbitrage operations between the IMM and interbank market would then be impossible.

One of the most popular IMM currency contracts has been the Deutsche mark. The IMM's comparative advantage over banks in markets where spot and forward dealing is particularly complimentary does not apply to trading the Deutsche mark but even there the IMM technology is still better suited to small size transactions (see *Money, Hard and Soft*, chapter 3). Small businesses and speculators can often deal more cheaply in mark-dollar futures on the IMM than in the interbank market. Only in markets such as the Mexican peso, however, where dealing in forwards and spot is not highly complimentary, can the IMM hope to gain a major share of wholesale trade.

Challenging established futures markets

Creating a market is a risky venture. Many of the new contracts introduced in commodity exchanges during the 1970s were a failure. Copper on the IMM, gold on the Chicago Board of Trade, commercial paper futures on the Chicago Board of Trade, zinc on New York Comex are all examples of contracts that failed to excite trading interest. Currencies, gold, and T-Bills on the IMM, pork bellies on Chicago's Mercantile Exchange, GNMA futures on the Chicago Board of Trade, are examples of spectacular successes in contract innovation during the same period.

The factors responsible for success or failure in futures contract innovation are probably as diverse as for success in any human endeavour. Some attempt may be made nevertheless to discern some general principles.

It is extremely difficult to introduce a contract which is already actively traded elsewhere into a given market. For example, copper has been for a long time traded in Comex (New York). An established broker and dealer network and clientele assure a liquid market there, with low bid-offer spreads. Why should anyone instruct their broker to fulfil their order in Chicago, rather than Comex, when in the new Chicago market there is as yet no assurance of liquidity? The only incentives to do so could be if brokerage commissions were much lower or if the form of contract (delivery dates, unit size, etc.) was preferable.

Despite the obstacles to new entry, two markets have introduced successfully contracts competitive with those established already elsewhere. First, the Board of Trade in Chicago launched successfully a silver contract in competition with Comex. The contract was differentiated from the Comex one, by having delivery dates in alternate months. The date of introduction, 1969, was fortunate: a free gold market for other than official transactions had just been established the year previously, and inflation fervour was gathering. A shock change to the financial system can be a basis for new market formation, as the earthquake of war can bring new nations into existence. Again in 1975, the legitimisation of American trading in gold, was the occasion of the successful launching of gold contracts both on the IMM and on Comex.

The soyabean oil market on the Chicago Board of Trade is the second example of a contract launched successfully in competition with an established market. Turnover was boosted initially by various scandals that had hit the New York market.

New contracts, unlike new products, cannot be patented. But the successful contract innovator seems well protected against new entrants. A challenger in another market place must assure a critical level of liquidity before he can hope usually to gain custom. Yet liquidity itself depends on a high volume of turnover. The challenger could break the vicious circle by himself guaranteeing liquidity at above that level economically supportable in the early stages. The exchange in which the competing contract is launched could limit strictly at first the number of market-makers and insist that their bid-offer spreads do not exceed a set maximum. In return, these first market-makers would be awarded some equity interest in the contract, for example, the right to sell their market-making permits and be awarded a proportion of the sale price of further permits issued in the future. As yet, this method of contract promotion has not been tried.

Creating a new futures contract

Creation is highest risk when market-makers in the new market cannot quote at the start on a satellite basis to other already liquid markets. Indeed market-making in the early days of currency futures trading on the IMM was helped by the potential for dealers to 'lay off' positions in the interbank market. The possibility of such satellite creation assured to participants that bid-offer spreads were limited on the IMM.

The 90-day T-Bill futures contract on the IMM was backed from its beginning by liquidity in the existing cash markets. An active sale-and-repurchase market between banks and dealers exists in New York for maturities up to one year. A dealer in T-Bill futures can so offset a short position in three-month contracts by buying a six-month T-Bill spot, and selling it spot-and-buying-it-back three months forward. Similarly he can offset usually a long position in the three-month contract by buying-a-six-month-T-Bill-spot-and-selling-it three months forward (in a single reverse sale and repurchase agreement) and selling the bill immediately spot. In periods when trading in T-Bill futures was light, the possibility of such methods of satellite creation guarantees a minimum level of liquidity in the T-Bill futures market. The new market's long run success depended though, on developing sufficient turnover, so that direct market-making on the IMM was cheaper than what a client could achieve by matching deals elsewhere.

Both the T-Bill futures and currency futures innovations, while to some extent competitive with existing cash or interbank markets, did not compete directly with other futures markets. It was hoped that clients would be attracted by the low level of transaction cost and the peculiar features of organized futures trading offered compared to existing conventional markets.

The pork bellies market on the Chicago Mercantile Exchange is the only major example of the successful launching of a contract which has lacked the back-stop of satellite quotation from existing markets. The promoters of the pork bellies contract realized that many producers and consumers wished to hedge price risk, but were unable to do so. The innovators succeeded in attracting high volume turnover from an early date, having sold the idea of the market to major likely participants before its opening.

Chicago is the world's leader in futures contract innovation. In the years ahead attempts will be made to launch contracts in euro-dollar CDs, the Wall Street index, and many others. Success will depend doubtless on many random factors not listed here. The science of contract innovation is in an infant stage, and should grow steadily as the time-span of experience lengthens.

6 Dollar Commonwealth

For some international money investors, the late 1970s could have been described as the 'Great Deflation'. An Italian, whose favoured money was Swiss francs and whose monetary wealth was held predominately in francs, would have perceived a falling price for the Italian shopping basket. Possibly less than 100 miles distant, in Geneva, a less fortunate investor may have experienced the worst inflation of his lifetime. A Geneva resident whose favourite money was US dollars would have perceived a rocketing price for his shopping basket.

Inflation is in reality a highly personalized concept. Chapter 2 described how money polytheists constructed their standard of value as a combination of international monies, say US $ 50 per cent, Dm 25 per cent, Swiss fr. 25 per cent. The polytheist's perceived inflation rate is then the rate of increase in price of his particular shopping basket, where price is measured in terms of his chosen combination unit of account.

The commonwealth of dollar users extends far beyond the US. Dollar inflation measured in terms of the goods bought by the European can deviate substantially from the domestic US inflation rate. Such deviations, brought about by real exchange rate changes of the dollar, are shown in this chapter to be a key adjustment mechanism correcting imbalance in the offshore dollar markets. Further, the structure and fragilities of the international banking system servicing offshore users of national monies are explored.

INTERNATIONAL DIMENSION OF MONEY GROWTH

US banks supply dollar desposits and loans worldwide. The conventional framework of monetary analysis does not incorporate global supply and demand functions, but assumes that money is national not only in creation but also in utilization. At end-1978, offshore non-bank dollar deposits accounted approximately for 27 per cent of domestic US money supply (M2). Offshore non-bank deposits in marks and Swiss francs were around 8 and 12 per cent respectively of domestic money supply (M2) in West Germany and Switzerland respectively.

Supply and demand of offshore dollars

The suppliers of offshore dollars are the international banks. The banks' supply of offshore dollar deposits (measured in nominal terms) may be considered a function of two main variables; first, the stock of US high-powered money; second, the profitability of intermediation in euro-dollar banking.

The hypothesis of a systematic relation between the stock of US high-powered money and the supply of offshore dollar deposits rests on banks, in aggregate, having a stable demand function for monetary base as a proportion of their outstanding deposits worldwide.

For a given size of US monetary base, banks will change their target expansion rates for offshore dollar deposit and loan business according to the expected profits from intermediation. In the aftermath of the OPEC price rise of 1973–4, the demand for intermediation services in dollars jumped, as OPEC surpluses had to be lent to oil consuming nations. Yet at first the labour and capital capacity of the international banks were fixed, and margins between borrowing and lending rates rose sharply. Higher margins encouraged established banks to expand their operations, opening new offices and taking on new staff: new banks and financial centres also mushroomed. In the expansion, US banks were prominent.

The banking industry over-estimated the rate of growth in demand for their intermediation services. OPEC surpluses and oil consumer deficits declined steadily during 1976–8. The short-run response to over-capacity in any industry is price-cutting, as capacity shrinkage is a long-term adjustment. Thus international bank lending margins slumped during 1977–8. By cutting margins borrowing was encouraged internationally, predominately in dollars. One principal type of client was the sovereign borrower on a long-term syndicated credit basis. The rate of growth of supply of deposits and loans was so maintained at 1975–6 levels, when measured in nominal dollar terms (see table 6.1).

Demand for offshore dollar deposits should be specified in real terms. In practice the price deflator chosen should be a dollar index of world traded goods, because of the global spread of consumption by offshore money holders. Demand for offshore dollar deposits, so measured in real purchasing power terms, is a function of three main variables. First, the transactions demand for dollars is related to the volume of world trade. Second, the larger is the superiority of interest rates on dollars

Table 6.1   Offshore dollars in Europe and US money supply (M2)

End year	Offshore dollars		US money supply	
	$ bn	% pa	$ bn	% pa
1970	58.70	27.1	453.0	12.4
1971	70.75	20.5	507.0	11.9
1972	96.73	36.7	570.0	12.4
1973	131.38	35.8	634.0	11.2
1974	156.43	19.1	693.0	9.3
1975	189.47	21.1	739.0	6.6
1976	230.04	21.4	797.0	7.8
1977	272.88	18.6	874.0	9.7

Notes: (1) Source: Bank for International Settlements.
(2) Figures for offshore dollars relate only to euro-dollars.
Dollars in Nassau, Singapore and Bahrain etc. are excluded.
(3) Figures include interbank positions.

over those on competing monies, the greater is the demand for dollar deposits offshore, where substitutability between international monies offshore is higher than onshore. Third, the greater is the supposed volatility of the dollar price index of world manufactured goods compared to the volatility of the same index measured in Swiss francs, or Deutsche marks, the smaller will be the demand for offshore dollar deposits: other offshore monies increase in attractiveness as stores of value.

Disequilibrium offshore

If arbitrage by banks is not impeded between offshore and onshore money markets, the flexibility of interest rate differentials between the two is very narrow. Hence disequilibrium offshore unaccompanied by significant onshore disequilibrium cannot be corrected by interest rate adjustment alone. Instead the restoration of overall balance in domestic and offshore dollar markets requires a dollar exchange rate change.

The above principle of adjustment may be illustrated for the 1976–8 period. It is likely that the rate of growth of demand for real offshore dollar deposits slowed as the three main influences on demand moved unfavorably. First, the volume growth of world trade slowed sharply. Second, the real level of dollar interest rates was, in the short-term, held at a low level by continued Federal Reserve intervention in the US money market to resist rising rates. Third, the increased doubts about

Federal Reserve determination to control monetary growth encouraged the belief that marks may be a better store of value than dollars.

Yet the rate of supply of offshore dollar deposits did not slow. Conditions of excess capacity prevailed in the banking industry. Further, banks could not switch rapidly the denomination of their intermediation from dollars into marks: for reasons explained in chapter two, international borrowers are more attached than lenders to the dollar standard.

In the short run, equilibrium in the offshore dollar market was restored by a sharp rise in the dollar price index of world traded goods or equivalently, a fall in the dollar exchange rate. The rise in the dollar index of traded goods was sharper than of domestic US goods because offshore dollar growth was more excessive than onshore.

The greater external than internal depreciation of the dollar represents a real exchange rate change, which has an impact on the current account of the US balance of payments. As the current account improves and moves into surplus, offshore dollars come onshore. They are swept there by the rest of the world which in aggregate spends in the US their initial excess offshore dollar balances. At that time, the rate of growth of dollar money held by US residents, fuelled by inward payments, accelerates to exceed the rate of growth of dollar balances held by the rest of the world. The rate of dollar inflation in the US then surpasses the rate of increase of the dollar index of world traded goods. In long run equilibrium, the real dollar exchange rate will have returned to its initial level. Some of the offshore dollar inflation will have been swept onshore, reversing in part the initial excess inflation offshore.

Speculation and automation

The story, just related about the origin of international dollar inflation and how inflation offshore is transmitted onshore, has one missing chapter, entitled 'The Dollar Speculator'. Yet, its omission should have been guessed when mention was made of a real exchange rate change and subsequent adjustment in the current account of the balance of payments. The speculator should realize initially that there is a greater proportionate excess supply of dollars offshore than onshore, and that in the long run a cumulative improvement in the US current account is necessary if balance is to be restored both in onshore and offshore markets. Speculative operations ensure that the initial depreciation of the dollar is not greater than that required to generate the current account improvement, and provide a reasonable risk premium. If greater, the speculator would buy up part of the excess offshore dollar deposits in exchange for foreign currencies. He would intend to sell the dollars, to be used for payment against US net exports, when the current account improvement materializes.

Offshore money supply targets?

The Federal Reserve could prevent the eventual coming onshore of excess offshore dollars from influencing domestic monetary growth by increasing its open market operations in the US money market. A domestic squeeze would then be the cost of offshore dollar excesses in earlier years.

It may, however, be more satisfactory for the cycle of offshore ease followed by domestic squeeze to be avoided. A means would be required of identifying an excessive imbalance between offshore dollar demand and supply in its early stages. Given inevitable delays and imprecision in the collection of euro-market data, an early-warning system based on statistical revelations would be inefficient. Instead, sharp real depreciation itself of the dollar should be used as an early warning signal of offshore excesses. The Federal Reserve would react to the signal by braking immediately the growth of US monetary base.

ALTERNATIVES TO THE EURO-BANK

In order to appraise how a seizing up of the international banking system, such as might occur from growing apprehension about loan defaults, would affect the international economy, it is necessary to understand the unique features of bank intermediation. Five main features are demonstrated here; the provision of credit guarantees, odd-lot trading, marketing, stand-by facilities, and non-quoted loan investment.

Credit guarantees

Banks' assets consist principally of loans. A proportion of the loan portfolio is backed by shareholders' funds. The remainder is financed by issuing bank deposits and sometimes longer term notes. A depositor with a bank buys essentially a share of its managed loan portfolio, with a guarantee to the extent of paid-up capital provided by the bank shareholders. Equity capital in the bank backs the promise to redeem deposits at par when they mature. The price of the guarantee is the margin between the deposit rate and the average loan rate, net of administration expenses.

The greater is the proportion of bank borrowing that is long-term, the greater is the guarantee provided to short-term depositors, and the lower should be the cost of deposit finance. However, the more that bank equity holders share their guarantee function with loan stock holders, the lower is their expected return to capital. Long-term lenders to the bank will obtain some share of the fee obtained for guaranteeing short-term bank deposits.

In recent years euro-banks have issued floating rate notes (frns) of maturities varying between five and fifteen years, with the intention of maintaining the ratio of long-term funds to bank deposits. Frn holders have earned a fee for sharing a guarantee function with the bank shareholders: the return on frns has in general been $\frac{1}{4}$ per cent higher than the rate at which the bank offers euro-dollars in the interbank market.

Odd-lot dealing

Active non-bank dealer markets exist in credit and foreign exchange. The commercial paper market and Chicago IMM provide services that are in some degree substitutable for those provided by banks. Banks specialize in dealing in odd-lots and for odd dates. Commercial paper and bills are transacted in round amounts: bank deposits may readily be placed in any magnitude. Bills and currency futures have standardized maturity dates: banks, in contrast, will quote deposit and currency rates for any maturity.

The money market equivalent of inter-dealer trading in commodity futures or securities is the interbank market. Unlike in an organized futures market, inter-market-maker business between euro-banks is in general unsecured. Mutual credit assessment is continuous. Banks can borrow normally in the interbank market at rates below the prime borrowing cost for non-bank corporations. Suppose the three-month interbank dollar quote is $10-10\frac{1}{8}$ per cent. Whereas in the course of its dealing operations a bank could be offered funds by another at $10\frac{1}{8}$ per cent, a prime corporation would borrow at a small margin above that. The basis for the cheaper cost to the bank is two-fold. First, the bank has an additional equity shelter to the corporation. Second, interbank borrowing in the course of market-making operations is likely to be reversed quickly: in no way is such borrowing a permanent component of the bank's financing structure.

Where a bank uses the interbank market as a permanent source of finance, rather than as a transitory offset in the process of market-making, the rate charged would be higher than the offer rate of $10\frac{1}{8}$ per cent quoted above, possibly by as much as $\frac{1}{4}$ per cent. During part of the 1970s, Japanese banks were persistent net borrowers from the London interbank dollar deposit market. They paid rates above the average interbank offer quotes.

Providing credit lines

The bank credit market is unique in the provision of standby facilities. It is impossible, given the variability of cash flows, to estimate precisely net financing requirement, even on a daily basis. By arranging standby facilities, or credit lines, corporations can meet unpredictable financing requirements at zero notice. In contrast, in the commercial paper or bill market, new issues take time to arrange.

Banks can provide credit lines to commercial customers by arranging mutual credit lines among themselves. Euro-banks in general arrange credit lines with major New York banks who are members of the clearing house for euro-dollar transactions. The New York banks establish mutual lines with each other.

Marketing specialists

Banks issue deposits and sell loans continuously. They have an established network of customers, and direct effort towards establishing on-going relations. They enjoy economies in marketing debt not obtainable by the corporation attempting to issue short-term debt either directly, or through a security house. The house must incur usually the expense of auctioning a commercial paper issue – the market must be called into existence (see chapter 5, p. 107). In contrast, the market in bank deposits operates continuously during business hours, and the bank can finance quickly a new loan arranged for a corporation by increasing its deposit issue.

Despite the comparative marketing advantage of the bank, large commercial paper markets are found in the US, although not in the euro-dollar market. In the US, reserve requirements impose a tax on bank intermediation, and so it is sometimes cheaper to borrow directly by issuing paper than indirectly from the banking system.

Non-quoted loan investment

Many borrowers are too small to create a liquid market in their own debt. High volume of turnover in the debt is not possible, and dealing spreads would be very wide in the secondary market. Auctioning paper would be very expensive, as the particulars of a small corporation or country are unlikely to be known widely.

Banks are specialists in the buying of such non-marketable debts, which may nevertheless be of top credit quality. Their loan departments are trained to appraise the risks of borrowers. Even a low risk small borrower pays some price, in the form of higher margin, for the natural illiquidity of his debts.

FAULTS OF ASYMMETRY

In subsistence economies complete symmetry exists between producer and consumer. The self-sufficient farmer and his family eat all his production. No imbalance can grow between supply and demand; a decision to increase production is simultaneous with a decision to increase consumption. Business cycles are a cost of asymmetry between producer and consumer that is an inevitable outcome of the division of labour according to comparative advantage.

In currency markets, it has been demonstrated already how an asymmetrical shift in preference by borrowers and lenders between international monies is a source of exchange rate disturbance (see p. 60). The greater proportion of borrowers than lenders that are institutions explains why lenders are typically readier to switch from using dollars to other international units of account.

In the money markets, preferences of borrowers and lenders are not symmetrical either in choice of banking institution or financial centre. Some banks and financial centres attract more loan than deposit non-bank business while others find the reverse. A proportion of interbank flows are long-term in nature, going from centres and banks with a comparative advantage in deposit taking to those with a comparative advantage in loan making. Any interruption to these flows is shown here to be a potential source of turbulence in the world money market.

Specialization in banking

Small euro-banks must pay typically higher interest on dollar deposits than large US branch competitors. The small bank does not have the same supposed degree of access to Federal Reserve facilities. Even if the small and large bank had identical loan portfolios outstanding, the large bank would be regarded as being of lower risk by depositors and would borrow at a cheaper rate.

The small bank needs to look for business in specialist areas, developing expertise in certain types of loan business and deposit taking. In practice, small banks seem better equipped to develop specialist advantage in non-bank loan than deposit business. Many small banks are in effect finance companies, borrowing in the interbank market to finance a portfolio of specialist, and often higher than average risk loans.

Relying on interbank loans as a permanent source of finance is high risk. During a credit squeeze, the large banks will cut back first in the low profit areas of their loan business, interbank loans in particular. Margins on interbank lending to one-way banks will increase, cutting back their profits substantially. Hence small bank profits are more cyclical than are those of large banks. Small banks may protect themselves against greater volatility of earnings by maintaining a higher capital-deposit ratio than their larger competitors.

Large American banks themselves operate sometimes as small one-way banks in domestic money markets outside the US. For example, US banks in Italy have developed loan business in liras which is complimentary to their euro-currency business with large Italian corporations. The US banks have no natural deposit base in lire, and borrow largely in the interbank lira market from domestic Italian banks. During credit squeezes interbank rates on liras have risen as much as 3 per cent above non-bank deposit rates, as the opportunity cost of funds lent interbank increases.

Asymmetries between financial centres

New financial centres developed fast in the 1970s, Bahrain and Singapore being principal examples. Both centres had one-way tendencies, having many more non-bank loan than deposit customers. A high proportion of loans were financed by borrowing in the London interbank market. The greater development of loan business can be explained by the evident economies in loan administration from being within easier reach of the borrower's business. There is not a similar size economy in administering deposits placed by nearby compared to far distant customers.

The new financial centres are particularly vulnerable to credit squeezes in a major offshore or domestic US money market because of their dependence on interbank finance. Similarly to the small bank, the small centre would find that the cost of interbank financing would rise more sharply than non-bank finance, which is in poor supply. Unless the new centres can grow to a stage of achieving better balance between their loan and deposit business, they will continue to be regarded as a high risk fringe of major European and North American centres.

Climatology of financial centres

We all know that the pattern of vegetation worldwide is determined by physical climatic conditions. It is less well known that the pattern of financial market-making is influenced heavily by political climatic conditions.

International financial centres can flourish only in politically temperate zones. Consider an attempt to develop Rome, situated in a hot political climate, into a major financial centre. A euro-bank in Rome would have to pay a higher deposit rate on dollars than a similar size bank in London which had an identical risk portfolio and an identical capital-deposit ratio. Even if both had lent entirely to corporations of top credit status (AAA) in Switzerland and the US, the perceived risk of the Italian bank would be higher due to the political risk of expropriation. The difference between the rates paid to finance identical loan portfolios by the London and Rome bank decreases as the loans become riskier. For example if the loans of both the London and Rome bank were almost entirely to LDCs, the risk differential between the two banks perceived by depositors would be slight.

A high political risk centre cannot compete with a low risk one in making top quality loans. At best, the high risk centre may trade on its comparative advantage of lending in high risk areas. A top-rated borrower should borrow only from top rated banks in top rated centres. Any other strategy would involve his paying a premium to lenders for a risk which he need never have assumed.

EURO-ARMAGEDDON

The 1970s were years of very rapid growth in the euro-markets. Hegelians would argue that growth is followed inevitably by a period of withdrawal. Further, the seeds of decay should be identifiable already in the years of advance. An attempt is made here to illustrate two disasters that could befall the euro-markets.

Massive default by LDCs

Post-1973 international bank lending to the less developed world increased sharply, as part of the process of intermediation between OPEC surpluses and LDC deficits. Some forecasts of euro-market disaster are based on massive default by over-stretched LDCs. Interbank borrowing and lending would then seize up as banks became unwilling to lend to each other. Interbank dealing is an essential component of market-making, and its interruption would cause a crisis of liquidity. Bid-offer spreads in deposit and foreign exchange markets would widen considerably. Further, bankruptcies would spread among banks which depended on interbank financing.

In reality, a euro-market crisis could erupt well before LDC default became massive. It would be sufficient for substantial non-bank depositors to become seriously concerned that the proportion of bank loans of poor credit rating outstanding to LDCs was very high. Simultaneously depositors would re-appraise the risk of banks relative to other corporations. Large American banks with heavy LDC exposure may come to be regarded as only of A or AA risk instead of AAA⁺. (In the USA, various credit agencies rank corporations according to their risk of default on loans. Lowest risk is AAA, followed by AA, then A, then BBB, then BB, etc.). The basis of decline in credit-rating of banks would be two-fold. First, the rating of banks' loan portfolios would be revised downwards. Second, bank profitability would deteriorate. Many of the loans to LDCs are long-term, at fixed margins, and so the banks could be committed to lending for many years to come at below revised market rates.

The overhang of cheap loans would reduce the capacity of banks to lend to AAA customers. Prime borrowers would find it cheaper to raise finance directly in the open market, rather than by using bank intermediation services. The now A or AA rated bank's marginal cost of deposits to on-lend to an AAA customer could be higher than the rate on AAA commercial paper. The residue of bad loans would place the bank in a position analogous to that of the high political risk financial centre that cannot lend profitably in safe areas.

Decomposition of bank loan portfolios into collections of second rate loans is not inevitable. Banks could restore their AAA status by seeking a new injection of equity capital. The old shareholders would bear the windfall loss incumbent on the market's marking down of the credit rating of bank loan portfolios. Providing confidence can be maintained, or restored, in the quality of bank management, the bank should be able to raise new equity capital. The higher ratio of capital reserves to deposits outstanding would compensate for the overhang of bad loans in the credit assessment of bank depositors.

Change in political climate

Suppose that London, the centre of the euro-markets, was to become politically risky. Historically that occurred in the late 1930s, when the outbreak of war was feared in Europe, and funds sought a safer home in the US. In a similar situation today, euro-dollar interest rates would shoot up relative to those in the US, as the risk of inconvertibility in Europe increased. Yet London banks would have loans outstanding to borrowers outside the European area. Such borrowers would find it profitable to repay their euro-dollar loans and refinance in politically more secure centres, probably in the US. The size of the euro-dollar market would shrink rapidly. On the assumption that Europeans themselves would consider the risk of euro-dollar deposits to have increased, interest rates in the shrunken euro-dollar market would remain high above those in the growing refuge centres.

Futurity

The 1970s were years of rapid growth of international financial markets. The US dollar was pre-eminent in the world money order, peace and political stability reigned in Europe, and banking institutions were apparently sound.

In the early chapters it was shown how the spectre of persistently worse inflation performance in the US compared to West Germany is ushering in an age of bi-polarism in the currency markets. Swings in the dollar-mark axis cause currencies in the dollar and mark orbits to move in similar direction to their respective poles. In earlier ages, men throughout the world had a common conception of monetary value, gold. For almost three decades after the second World War, the US dollar achieved universal acceptance. In the age of bi-polarism, people in West and East hemispheres dream in different monies.

The temple of Dollar International has been supported by the twin pillars of US economic strength and the worldwide banking industry. There are faults in its foundations. Acceleration of US inflation or panic about the soundness of banks could subject Dollar International to stress. The direction of shockwaves would emanate through markets far beyond the site of the initial eruption. No doubt there would be a successor temple, but it would be of inferior quality to Dollar International built on the base of low inflation in the US.

Bibliography

Chapter 1

Clarke, Stephen V. O. 'Exchange Rate Stabilization in the Mid-1930s: Negotiating the Tripartite Agreement' *Princeton Studies in International Finance*, No. 41 (1977).

Mundell, Robert A. 'A Theory of Optimum Currency Areas' *American Economic Review*, 60, No. 4 (September 1961) pp. 657–65.

Rhomberg, R. R. 'Indices of Effective Exchange Rates' *IMF Staff Papers*, (March 1976).

Vaubel, Roland. 'Real Exchange Rate Changes in the European Economic Community: The Empirical Evidence and its Implications for European Currency Unification' *Weltwirtschaftliches Archiv Review of World Economics*, (December 1976) No. 3, pp. 429–470.

Chapter 2

Aliber R. Z. *Exchange Risk and Corporate International Finance* (London: Macmillan, 1978).

Ascheim, Joseph and Park, Y. S. 'Artificial Currency Units: the formation of functional currency areas' *Princeton Essays in International Finance*, No. 114 (April 1976).

Giddy, Ian H. and Gunter Dufey. 'The Random Behavior of Flexible Exchange Rates: Implications for Forecasting' *Journal of Business Studies*, 6 (Spring 1975) pp. 1–32.

Poole, William 'Speculative Prices as Random Walks: An Analysis of Ten Time Series of Flexible Exchange Rates' *Southern Economic Journal*, 33 (April 1967) pp. 468–478.

Solnik, Bruno H. 'An Equilibrium Model of the International Capital Market' *Journal of Economic Theory*, 7 (August 1974) pp. 500–524.

Chapter 3

Aliber R. Z. 'Exchange Risk, Political Risk, and Investor Demand for

External Currency Deposits' *Journal of Money, Credit, and Banking*, 7, No. 2 (May 1975) pp. 161–180.

Aliber R. Z. 'The IRPT: A Re-interpretation' *Journal of Political Economy*, 6 (November 1973) pp. 1451–59.

Aliber R. Z. 'The Firm under Pegged and Flexible Exchange Rates' *Scandinavian Journal of Economics*, 78 (May 1976) pp. 309–22.

Lindert, Peter H. 'Key Currencies and Gold 1900–1913' *Princeton Studies in International Finance*, No. 24 (1969).

Officer L. H. 'The PPP Theory of Exchange Rates: A Review Article' *IMF Staff Papers*, 23 (March 1976) pp. 1–61.

Chapter 4

Barratieri, V. and Ragazzi, G. 'An Analysis of the Two-Tier Foreign Exchange Market' *Banca Nazionale del Lavoro Quarterly Review*, (December 1971) pp. 354–72.

Blejer, Mario I. 'Exchange Restrictions and the Monetary Approach to the Exchange Rate', in *Economics of Exchange Rates*, ed. Frenkel and Johnson, Addison. (Wesley, 1978).

Brown, Brendan D. 'Exchange Restrictions: their implications for portfolio management' *Economic Journal*, 87, No. 347 (September 1977) pp. 543–53.

Culberstson, William P. 'Purchasing Power Parity and Black Market Exchange Rates' *Economic Inquiry*, 13, No. 2 (May 1975) pp. 287–296.

Michaely, Michael 'A Geometrical Analysis of Black Market Behavior' *American Economic Review*, (Sept. 1954) pp. 627–637.

Pick, Franz '*Pick's Currency Yearbook*,' (New York, Various issues).

Sheckh, M. A. 'Black Market for Foreign Exchange, Capital Flows and Smuggling' *Journal of Development Economics*, 3, No. 1 (March 1976) pp. 9–26.

Chapter 5

Brown, Brendan D. 'A Clarification of the Interest Rate Parity Theorem' *European Economic Review*, 12 (September 1979).

Brown, Brendan D. 'The Forward Sterling Market and its Relation to Arbitrage between the Silver Market in London, Chicago, and New York' *Oxford Economic Papers*, 29 (July 1977) pp. 792–311.

Frenkel J. A. and Levich R. M., 'Covered Interest Arbitrage: Unexploited Profits?' *Journal of Political Economy*, 83 (April 1975) pp.

325–338. 'Transaction Costs and Interest Arbitrage: Tranquil versus Turbulent Periods' *Journal of Political Economy*, 85 (December 1977) pp. 1209–1226.

Marston, Richard C. 'Interest Arbitrage in the Euro-Currency Markets' *European Economic Review*, 7 (February 1976) pp. 1–14.

Chapter 6

Brown, Brendan D. 'Money in a Competitive Banking System' *Journal of Bank Research*, 7 (June 1976) pp. 179–183.

Dornbusch, Rudiger 'The Theory of Flexible Exchange Rate Regimes and Macroeconomic Policy' *Scandinavian Journal of Economics*, 78 (May 1976).

Goodhardt, Charles '*Money, Information and Uncertainty*' (Macmillan 1975).

Makin, John H. '*Eurocurrencies and the Evolution of the Internation Monetary System*' ed. Carl H. Stern, John H. Makin, and Dennis E. Logue (American Enterprise Institute, Washington DC, 1977) pp. 17–52.

McKinnon, Ronald I. 'The Euro-Currency Market' *Princeton Essays in International Finance*, No. 125 (December 1977).

Mussa, Michael 'The Exchange Rate, the Balance of Payments, and Monetary and Fiscal Policy under a Regime of Controlled Floating' *Scandinavian Journal of Economics*, 78 (May 1976) pp. 229–248.

Willett, Thomas D. 'Discussion: Euro-dollars, Speculation and Foreign Exchange' *Journal of Money, Credit and Banking* (August 1972) pp. 636–642.

Index

Index